Strategies for
STRUGGLING
LEARNERS
A Guide for the Teaching Parent

Strategies for STRUGGLING LEARNERS

A Guide for the Teaching Parent

Joe P. Sutton, Ph.D.
Connie J. Sutton, M.A.Ed.

Exceptional Diagnostics

220 Douglas Drive • Simpsonville, SC 29681

Exceptional Diagnostics

Cover Design: Brian D. Johnson
Typesetting: Thomas H. Juchum, Richard R. Roth
Production Manager: Don Mauk
Printer: Bob Jones University Print Shop
Cover Photography: Unusual Films (large),
       John Nolan (Inset, back)

Product Acknowledgment: Student in the front cover foreground photograph is using *Hands-On Equations*®, a patented teaching methodology developed by Dr. Henry Borenson for introducing basic algebraic concepts.

Library of Congress Catalog Card Number: 95-90291

Recommended Cataloging in Publication Data

Sutton, Joe P. (Joe Perry), 1956-
    Strategies for struggling learners: a guide for the
teaching parent / Joe P. Sutton, Connie J. Sutton
        p. cm.
    Includes bibliographical references and index.
    ISBN 0-9645684-0-3
    1. Special education—United States. 2. Home
schooling. I. Sutton, Connie J., 1956– . II. Title.
          1995
    371.9'26—dc20   95-90291
                                  CIP

Printed in the United States of America
10 9 8 7 6 5 4 3 2 1

DEDICATION

To our sons, Jeremy, Jason, and Jared, who patiently endured while Mom and Dad struggled to write this book.
We will always love you.

TABLE OF CONTENTS

IEP

CHAPTER 11   (Educational Procedures) 151

Record Keeping

PREFACE

For too many years, parents of struggling learners have had to depend largely on learning specialists in conventional schools and so-called "therapists" in clinical settings in order to get the help these children needed. In fact, some professionals still arrogantly contend that "parents can't be expected to know"[1] how to help their own children. We reject this view, and believe to the contrary that parents are quite capable of teaching their own children, regardless of limitations in learning, attention, and/or behavior that the children may have. This book, presented in twelve chapters, seeks to equip parents with the *strategies* (i.e., "plans of action") and practical tools they will need to be more successful in this endeavor.

In Chapter 1, we introduce parents to a *Formula for Success*, which includes ten guidelines for effectively teaching struggling learners. We discuss *Learners with Limitations* in Chapter 2 and provide a brief overview of the more prevalent disabilities found among many children today who struggle. In Chapter 3, we help parents establish a basic core of *Essential Teaching Beliefs* that finds its roots in five basic Scriptural principles. We search God's Holy Word further in Chapter 4 to discover how Christ Jesus, the Master Teacher, taught those who had limitations, and delineate a *Scriptural Model for Teaching* struggling learners that parents can follow.

We devote Chapter 5 to a discussion of the basic essentials of *Testing and Evaluation* that apply to children with disabilities and others who struggle. In Chapter 6, we help parents understand the importance of developing a *Blueprint for Instruction* or an individualized education plan (IEP) which should steer the design of tailor-made home instruction for struggling learners. *Consultant Services* are discussed in Chapter 7, which includes recommendations on how to secure a consultant when the need arises. Chapter 8 focuses on *Modifying Instruction* in the home, with suggestions on how parents can modify both the learning environment and their own teaching behavior.

We introduce numerous *Generic Teaching Techniques* in Chapter 9 that parents can use to teach just about any subject. In Chapter 10, we concentrate on specialized teaching *Techniques for Specific Subjects*, particularly those methods that have been found to be effective in teaching reading, spelling, and mathematics to struggling learners. We address the topic of *Educational Procedures* in Chapter 11, where parents can find helpful suggestions on how to set up a daily teaching schedule, how to compile a permanent folder, and so on. Finally, Chapter 12 describes various techniques for *Managing Student Behavior*, which parents may need to implement in order to make learning more efficient for struggling learners.

We would be amiss if we failed to recognize the following individuals who spent countless hours reviewing our book: Tom and Sherry Bushnell, Nationally Challenged Homeschoolers Associated Network; Inge Cannon, Executive Director, Education PLUS™, Sharon Grimes, national convention speaker, Dr. Carl Herbster, President, American Association of Christian Schools, and Scott W. Somerville, Esq., Home School Legal Defense Association. Their wise counsel and helpful suggestions were invaluable.

It has taken almost two years to complete this project. The Lord has truly been our Strength during those moments when it seemed like the words would not come. By His grace, we have not wavered in our mission—that parents have a reliable, trustworthy resource of ideas on how to teach struggling learners in the home. Our prayer is that parents will implement these *Strategies for Struggling Learners*, and that they will receive encouragement from these pages to keep on keeping on.

JPS & CJS

Beechick, R. (1991), p. 49

Strategies for STRUGGLING LEARNERS

A Guide for the Teaching Parent

Chapter 1

FORMULA FOR SUCCESS

B ooks about how to be successful abound today. Some of these books may be valid. Others are simply sham. The danger is that many well-meaning people fall prey to the unfounded ideas promoted in some of these books. More important, there seems to be a common message that permeates many of these success-oriented books. The message, although subtle at times, is simple...*You can obtain a lot in this life with little to no effort or work.* How beguiling and injurious this message is! Unfortunately, this "quick and easy...get something for nothing" philosophy has ruined many families in modern America. In truth, very few things of great value in this life can be obtained without hard work and immense effort.

So it is with teaching struggling learners. We would do our readers a great disservice if we were to suggest that teaching children with learning difficulties is an easy task, whether in a conventional school or at home. It is not. It stands to reason that struggling learners are complex individuals with very unique needs, and home instruction programs designed to meet their unique needs may be as complex and involved as the children themselves. Susan Parrish,[1] a home educating mother, declares, "I learned over time, [that] schooling an impaired child can take three times the energy, patience and knowledge and is not for the faint of heart." Even though teaching struggling learners will not be easy, parents can learn to do it well, if they are willing to invest the necessary time and effort to plan and make proper preparation.

Interestingly, some parents of struggling learners use grade level textbooks and workbooks from one or more of the leading, commercially-produced curricula in their home education efforts. Although a rare few may realize some limited success in this simplistic approach, there are many more parents in the long-run who testify that this way of trying to teach struggling learners is ineffective for the most part. We agree with Debbie Mills,[2] a home educating mother of a disabled child, who claims, "For many children with disabilities the traditional scope and sequence do not apply."

Trying to make standard curricular materials designed for typical, "average" children work for struggling learners is like forcing a square peg in a round hole. One mother of two exceptional children (i.e., developmental disability and gifted/talented), described her frustration with standard curricula this way: "We are indoctrinated that we must have approved professional curriculum when there are probably more differences in our children's learning than literature available."[3] Leaning totally on standard curricula for use with struggling learners generally produces only frustration for both parent and child. Simply put, standard curricula are not enough.[4] Parents of struggling learners must do more in the area of developing and planning *tailor-made* programs of instruction if these children are to succeed and reach their God-given potential. No doubt, tailor-making and developing an individualized home education program will require much work. But parents can do it!

We have developed a "formula for success" that parents can follow that should ease the burden of developing complex programs of instruction for struggling learners. Before we reveal our formula for success, though, let us share with you the testimony of one home educating mother whom we met a few years ago. We believe her testimony speaks volumes and represents the heartfelt feelings of many other parents across this great land who have children with learning difficulties:

> Our son, Bradley, is eighteen years old. He is a senior at a large Christian school in the Southeast. He was home schooled until his junior year....It was over a year ago that Bradley's English teacher sent a note home that said, "I

think Bradley has difficulty processing information." His first progress reports upon entering his senior year were mostly Ds. Yet he had been a B+ home school student. We could not understand what was happening. One of the reasons we missed Bradley's learning disability was his extreme giftedness in the areas of communication and analytical skills. He could do things around the house that were truly "exceptional" and so we overlooked some of his other learning problems and academic weaknesses.

The Christian school requested that Bradley be evaluated. The evaluator found that Bradley had something called a specific learning disability in spelling, reading comprehension, and mathematics. Although the meeting with the evaluator was less than encouraging, we found the response from the teachers at the Christian school to be warm and understanding. Most of Bradley's regular teachers admitted, however, that they did not know how to deal with a student that had a learning disability.

Since the Christian school did not have a special education resource program where Bradley could get specialized help for his disability, we had to employ a professional special educator to work with him after school hours several times per week. This has just opened up doors to what has been a very positive experience for our son. The special educator developed unique learning strategies that have allowed Bradley to learn more efficiently. He also made suggestions on how the regular classroom teachers could accommodate Bradley's learning disability and modify instruction/testing situations for him so that he could be able to show his best work.

It has been over a year and a half now since we discovered our son's learning disability. Bradley will be graduating in just a few months. You may be wondering how it is with him now. The progress has been phenomenal! He is now making Bs at the Christian school. He was selected as one of two students to represent his high school at Boys State, which is a federally/state funded summer camp experience for students demonstrating elevated leadership abilities. He has been selected for inclusion in "Who's Who Among American High School Students." He holds a school campus job where he has been appointed to supervise the work of thirty other students.

To go from where we were eighteen months ago to now has to do primarily with the Lord's goodness and a major change in our attitude about disabled students. Our son's special education teacher told us early on that, although we must recognize our son's weaknesses and limitations, we must not concentrate or dwell on them. We must accept him as he is, which is how the Lord created him, and to focus on his strengths and gifts. God has a way of turning a person's limitations into assets for His glory. And that is exactly what has happened. But we did have to secure special education intervention for him.

I never picked up on the fact that our son had a learning disability during his home school years. That is something that has and continues to bother me. Our son has two older siblings that are both graduating from college this year—a brother, 23 and a sister who is 21. They were home schooled, too, and studied the same basic college preparatory curriculum that Bradley did. Yet they have not struggled with their learning as Bradley has.[5]

Two basic emotions stir within us each time we read this mother's testimony. First of all, our hearts ache. We ache for this mother, and we ache for other parents who have students that need an individualized education and, for whatever reason, have not had access to one. Although this young boy went for years in the home school without ever being identified as disabled, his mother nonetheless did the best that she could and taught him based on what she thought he needed. For the most part, we believe she was successful in teaching him for those eleven years in the home school. No doubt, she is responsible for a great deal of the success he has and continues to experience.

But we wonder how *different* the home instruction would have been for Bradley had his mother known that he had a learning disability. It is clear that Bradley needed a highly individualized, tailor-made educational program, for once he entered the conventional Christian school setting, where he could not receive the individualization that he was getting in the home, he immediately began to fail. Bradley needed an educational program that was designed to meet his unique needs.

We ache, yes, but we also rejoice in our hearts and are thankful. We rejoice in the fact that God makes no mistakes (Ps. 18:30), and that this young boy's disability was not a blunder of a slumbering God (Ps. 121:3). We rejoice in the success of all those home school years and the success Bradley realized during his high school years in the conventional Christian school. We are thankful that Bradley, like all of us, had gifts that he was able to use for the glory of God. We are thankful that God used this young man, his disability notwithstanding, as a testimony of His grace, goodness, and power. What an example this home educated boy was and continues to be to others!

If Bradley's mother had known about his disability during those home school years, and could have provided him a tailor-made program of instruction, how might she have done it? We recommend the following ten guidelines in developing effective programs of instruction for struggling learners:

• Understand the child's characteristics and behaviors;
• Adopt essential teaching beliefs and principles;
• Follow a Scriptural model for teaching;
• Assess the child's abilities and progress regularly;
• Implement an individualized educational plan (IEP);
• Consult with professionals when necessary;
• Tailor teaching methods to the needs of the child;
• Develop proper educational procedures;
• Use appropriate behavior management techniques; and
• Commit the child's progress to the Lord.

We don't claim to have the perfect "formula for success." There may in fact be other guidelines that we have failed to include. Some parents may want to enhance or add their own ideas to our formula. We agree that these ten guidelines, at first glance, are almost overwhelming. But we wouldn't expect parents to master all of these over night. No doubt, the teaching parent will need to read and prepare properly in order for this formula to produce the desired success.

Integrating these guidelines gradually, one or two at a time, over the course of an entire school year may be the better route for the teaching parent who may have other children to care for. Others may only need a summer in advance to prepare. We do believe, though, that our formula may represent the minimum number of guidelines that are necessary for success. To the extent that parents master and integrate these guidelines in designing individualized home instruction for their children, they should expect to see success. The chapters that follow are devoted to explaining and illustrating in greater detail how the teaching parent can put these guidelines into practice.

---

[1]Parrish (1995), p. 42
[2]Mills (1995), p. 20
[3]Personal communication with authors, February 6, 1995.
[4]J. Sutton (1994b)
[5]J. Sutton (1994a)

Chapter

2

LEARNERS WITH LIMITATIONS

Perfection. Only the Lord Jesus Himself has experienced
perfection on this side of eternity, because He was and is
the only Perfect One that has ever walked the face of this planet.
Both the present and future of mankind would be dismally bleak,
though, if there were no hope of a life without sin and its consequences. But we know that the redeemed in Christ will be perfect
one day, for the Scripture promises that "we shall all be changed"
(I Cor. 15:51), and "we shall be like Him" (I John 3:2). As won-
derful as these truths are, we will nonetheless have to bear the
limitations the Lord has placed upon us while we remain on this
earth.

The limitations that most people will probably have to bear will
be little more than the usual basic aches, pains, and worries that
have accompanied every man and woman since Adam's fall. But
for some, limitations may involve diminished abilities and skills to
some degree. For example, some individuals have great difficulty
communicating publicly and cringe at the thought of having to
speak before an audience of more than two or three other people.
Yet these same individuals are generally able to express themselves
effectively on a one-on-one basis. Others may have two "left feet"
and lack the agility necessary to participate, even leisurely, in
sports and athletic activities. Yet these same people are quite
capable of walking and getting around in a day-to-day, routine way.

For a certain segment of our population, though, God allows
limitations of a more severe nature, typically called *disabilities*,

which may significantly impair their learning, behavior, emotional and/or physical capabilities. We believe that many struggling learners may have one or more forms of disability. Students with disabilities can be found in almost any educational setting—public schools, Christian schools, and home schools alike. What most people don't realize, is just how many students with disabilities there are in this country. The figures are startling.

According to the U.S. Department of Education,[1] a little more than 4.8 million children (or approximately 10% of the school age population) had some form of disability and were being served in public school special education classrooms during the 1990-91 school year. One may wonder whether this figure holds true for students in the home school population. Unfortunately, there are no reliable, published figures on the number/percentage of students in home schools who have disabilities. Nonetheless, Janet (Wayne) Walker[2] has estimated that approximately 5% of the home school population of students have disabilities of some sort. She bases this figure on information about children with disabilities supplied by the parents who hold membership with the Home School Legal Defense Association (HSLDA).

Interestingly, Walker's figure coincides with the percentage of students with documented disabilities found in fundamental Christian schools, which is between 4.8% and 5.5%.[3] We believe that this figure is probably not reflective of the *true* number of children with disabilities in Christian schools and that the actual figure is much closer to that reported above for public schools. Since Christian schools for the most part (94%) do not have formal special education programs in operation, it may well be that there are many students sitting in regular Christian school classrooms who have genuine disabling conditions, but have not been referred, evaluated, and identified properly. We believe the situation is similar in home schools across America. Since home education includes much individualized teaching, some parents may already be modifying and accommodating instruction for children who in reality differ significantly from the norm in learning, attention, and behavior, and would be classified as disabled if evaluated.

In short, we simply cannot deny the great numbers of struggling learners today with disabilities and their need for tailor-made programs of instruction. Moreover, we cannot be so shortsighted as to think that students with disabilities will only be found in public or private schools. God is no respecter of persons (Acts 10:34), and students with disabilities are found in home schools too. Parents who are part of the burgeoning home education movement in America must recognize students with disabilities for the unique creation that they are (Ps. 139:14). An important first step that must precede developing a tailor-made programs of instruction in the home school is understanding characteristics and behaviors of the various disabilities and how students with disabilities are properly identified.

Types of Disabilities

Drs. Daniel P. Hallahan and James M. Kauffman,[4] two of the leading scholars in the field of special education, describe eight major forms of exceptionality that children may have. They are as follows:

- communication (speech and language) disorders;
- emotional/behavior disorders;
- hearing impairments;
- giftedness;
- mental retardation;
- learning disabilities;
- physical/other health impairments; and
- visual impairments.

The most prevalent disability reported by the U.S. Department of Education[5] is learning disability, which represents almost half (49.1%) of all children with disabilities. Communication disorders, representing approximately one-fourth (22.7%) of the entire group of disabled children, comes in at second. Children with mental retardation (12.7%) and emotional/behavior disorders (9%) represent another sizeable proportion of the disabled student population, at third and fourth in rank order, respectively.

Interestingly, although the remaining disabilities have received considerably more media hype and attention that the other disabilities mentioned above, they represent only a very small percentage of the total group of students with disabilities. These include physical/other health impairments (2.4%), multiple disabilities (2.2%), hearing impairment (1.4%), and visual impairments (.5%). Unfortunately, federal officials do not include figures on children who are gifted and talented in their annual report to Congress, but the Office of Gifted and Talented in Washington has traditionally held that about 3% to 5% of the school population is gifted.[6]

Disabilities may range from mild to severe in the degree that they affect a child's ability to succeed in school work and behavior. What follows is a brief description of each of these disabilities. We refer our readers to a more comprehensive discussion of most of these disabilities in a book entitled, *Special Education: A Biblical Approach.*[7] See Appendix A for information on how to secure this book.

Learning Disabilities

The term "learning disability" was coined by Dr. Sam Kirk in the early 1960s and was officially defined by Congress in Public Law 94-142 in 1975. Prior to this time, many terms were used to describe this unique group of children including "minimal brain injury," "cerebral dysfunction," "central nervous system disorder," "conceptually handicapped," "perceptually handicapped," and "educationally handicapped," to name a few.

Although learning disabilities in children have only recently been recognized and acknowledged, while other disabilities such as retardation and blindness have been recognized for centuries, there have no doubt been individuals with learning disabilities since the beginning of time. Historical evidence proves that a number of important and famous people through the ages have had learning disabilities including Nelson Rockefeller, Thomas Edison, August Rodin, Woodrow Wilson, and Albert Einstein. Even more recently, the actor, Henry Winkler (who played the "Fonz" on the television sitcom, *Happy Days*), was identified as learning disabled during his grade school years.

Describing a learning disability (LD) can be difficult, since "symptoms are not the same from person to person."[8] That is, not all LD students demonstrate the same array of characteristic behaviors. What we do know for sure, though, is that the characteristics of LD students are numerous and varied. After analyzing a large group of LD students from across the country, Clements[9] identified the following ten most frequently found symptoms: hyperactivity, perceptual-motor problems, general coordination problems, emotional lability (frequent mood shifts), attention disorders, impulsivity, memory/thinking deficits, specific academic problems, speech/language/hearing problems, and neurological irregularities (abnormalities in brain activity). Learning disabled students may also demonstrate difficulties in information processing, learning strategy acquisition and usage, motivation, and social skills.[10,11]

The definition of specific learning disabilities adopted by the federal government in Public Law 94-142 and reiterated more recently in Public Law 101-476 (Individuals with Disabilities Education Act) has been the most commonly accepted standard for identifying LD students.[12] The definition is lengthy, laboriously worded, and even ambiguous in places, but from it we can glean the following key identifying criteria:

1. Normal/above normal intelligence. Perhaps one of the first distinguishing characteristics of virtually all LD students is that their intelligence scores generally fall within the normal range, that is, between 85 and 115.[13] It is clear that normal to above normal intelligence sets students with true learning disabilities apart from other students who have learning difficulties which may be stemming from subaverage, low intelligence. For example, students with mental retardation also have severe learning difficulties, but mentally retarded students by definition have intelligence quotients (IQs) that are below 70 to 75.

2. Underachievement in academic area(s). In addition to normal to above normal intelligence, students with learning disabilities will also demonstrate severe underachievement in one or more *academic* areas. In fact, academic problems are the most prominent, identifying characteristic of LD students. Hallahan and Kauffman[14] contend that "by definition, if there is no academic problem, a learning disability does not exist." The federal definition states that a child may have a specific learning disability in one or more of the following reading, language arts, and/or mathematics areas: (1) basic reading skills; (2) reading comprehension; (3) written expression (including spelling); (4) listening comprehension; (5) oral expression; (6) mathematics calculation; and (7) mathematics reasoning.

3. Discrepancy between intelligence and achievement. A number of leading authorities agree that the primary identifying criterion contained in the law for learning disabilities that is least disputed by scholars is establishment of "a severe discrepancy between [the child's] achievement and intellectual ability."[15] One's intellectual ability is simply one's God-given ability to think, reason, remember, process information, acquire knowledge, and learn. Intelligence is a reflection of a child's *potential* to learn. A child's achievement, on the other hand, is a reflection of what he has *actually* learned in academic areas and is typically measured by paper and pencil type tests.

Herein lies the great paradox with learning disabled children. Their normal to above normal intelligence suggests that they *should* be performing very satisfactory in academic work (i.e., As and Bs for those who grade conventionally) with little to no struggling. In reality, though, their school work and mastery of academic skills is at best only average and many times is below average and close to failing (i.e., Cs, Ds, and Fs). When parents ask examiners to eventually do a comprehensive evaluation of these children and administer one-on-one achievement tests, their achievement scores take a plunge as a reflection of their lack of mastery and success. Thus, what examiners must prove is that there is a mismatch or gap between the child's potential to learn (i.e., his intellectual ability) measured by intelligence tests, and his actual learning and performance (i.e., his achievement), measured by one-on-one achievement tests. This generally requires the use of statistical formulas.

4. Psychological processing problems. A third identifying criterion is that the LD child will show psychological processing problems. This simply means that the child will have difficulty with input and output of information that he receives during times of instruction and at other times. The end result is that the child generally will not efficiently and accurately produce the desired response, whether it be writing, speaking, pointing, moving, etc. Some students have problems processing visual information, while others have problems processing auditory information. Some may have problems in both areas.

Conventional classroom teachers generally can vouch that LD students have processing problems, for it can be detected quite easily when these students are required to take notes in class. The act of notetaking requires that the student process visual and/or auditory information as the teacher presents it. He must then quickly paraphrase the information while it is in his short-term memory and reproduce it in his own words as he writes it in his notebook. Parents may see similar difficulties in the home when they ask (which requires auditory processing) these children to complete an errand requiring multiple steps. Unfortunately, the child's failure to comply with parental commands many times is viewed as an act of disobedience (spiritual problem), when, in fact, the problem may be reflective of a processing weakness.

5. Not due to any other condition. Finally, the federal definition of learning disability makes it clear that a bona fide learning disability will be a distinct condition. The term *learning disability* will not apply to "children who have learning problems which are primarily the result of visual, hearing, or motor handicaps, of mental retardation, of emotional disturbance, or of environmental, cultural, or economic disadvantage."[16] Simply put, a true learning disability will not be the primary result of any other existing limitation. In short, then, the learning disability is a condition that stands alone and is the primary contributor to a child's serious learning problem.

We regret that some examiners today do not follow the federal government's definitional criteria for learning disability. It is not unusual to hear of a child who has been labeled as "visually learning disabled," "learning disabled in memory," or "learning disabled in attention." Informed parents will recognize immediately that these are not true learning disabilities, for visual, memory, and attention problems are not academic problems per se, but problems of a sensory/perceptual or cognitive nature. Moreover, these so-called learning disabilities are simply not recognized under the federal definition of learning disabilities. When examiners do not follow proper identifying criteria as they should, they may label students as learning disabled who really are not (which results in overidentification) or they may fail to label those students who actually have a true learning disability (which results in underidentification).

One term that has survived the years that is used synonymously with learning disabilities is "dyslexia," although it is becoming increasingly outdated. Dyslexia was a term that was coined in the early years of the special education movement in America and reflected a more medical, neurological orientation. The problem with using this term is that we cannot document neurological dysfunction in most learning disabled students, although we do presume it. Only in some severely learning disabled students can neurological dysfunction be proven. People today who still cling to the term *dyslexia* will nonetheless attest to the same typical reading decoding (i.e., pronunciation) and reading comprehension problems in these children that are described under the federal government's definition of learning disability in reading.

Parents should recognize the magnitude of the numbers of children nationwide who have learning disabilities. The likelihood of having a child with a learning disability is far greater than that of any other disability. As we mentioned earlier, almost half of all students identified as disabled are learning disabled. In comparison to other forms of disability, we now know that learning disabled students outnumber visually impaired students 98 to 1, hearing impaired students 35 to 1, students with multiple forms of disability 22 to 1, physically impaired students 20 to 1, emotional/behaviorally disordered students 5 to 1, mentally retarded students 4 to 1, and speech/language disordered students 2 to 1.[17]

Communication Disorders

Communication disorders represent some of the most disheartening of all disabilities. Imagine a child who is trying to communicate something to his parent or teacher, perhaps a need, and cannot because of a speech or language limitation. Children with communication disorders have just as much a need for special education as those children with specific learning disabilities, mental retardation, or other disability.

Communication disorders include serious problems in speech and/or language. A speech disorder means that the student has significant deficiencies in his ability to deliver and transmit intelligibly a message to his listeners. Language disorders, on the other hand, have to do with the actual message itself, not the mechanics of delivering the message. A child's inability to choose words carefully and to structure these words appropriately in sentences so that the intended meaning is conveyed to the listener is the essence of a language disorder.

Speech disorders come in three specific subtypes: (1) articulation; (2) voice; and (3) fluency problems. Speech disorders of articulation are by far the most prevalent, for approximately three-fourths of all speech disordered children have problems in articulation. Examples of articulation problems include substitutions (e.g., "wabbit" for rabbit), additions (e.g., "idear" for idea), omissions (e.g., "ba-ball" for baseball), and distortions (e.g., "ax" for ask).

Some children have voice speech disorders, which would include significant problems in voice quality (e.g., mellow, thin, hyponasal, or rough-sounding voices), pitch (e.g., monotone voices), and magnitude of sound (e.g., voices that are either too loud or too soft). Finally, some students will have speech disorders in fluency (called "dysfluencies"), stuttering being the most common type.[18]

Children with language disorders may show significant problems in use of phonemes (word sounds without meaning such as "ch"), morphemes (word sounds with meaning such as "*in*-ability"), syntax (rules of grammar and word usage), semantics (word meanings/relationships among words), and/or pragmatics (social use of language). Speech and language disorders are formally diagnosed by a speech/language pathologist.

Mental Retardation

Students with mental retardation share some of the same behavioral characteristics as LD students, including problems with attention, memory, organizing information, misbehavior (e.g., disruptiveness, distractibility), motivation, oral language, academic underachievement (especially reading), social skills (including self-esteem problems), emotional reactions and responses, and overall delayed development.[19,20]

Students classified as mentally retarded must meet three criteria: (1) subaverage intellectual functioning; (2) severe maladaptive behavior; and (3) manifestation of the condition between birth and 18 years of age. Subaverage intellectual functioning simply means that the child has an intelligence quotient (IQ) that is well below normal. Luckasson and his colleagues[21] have indicated that the American Association on Mental Retardation now requires that a student's IQ must be approximately 70 to 75 or below (remember, normal IQ ranges from 85 to 115) in order to qualify for classification as mentally retarded.

Adaptive behavior skills are "composed of a number of coping skills that, when combined, allow an individual to achieve community integration."[22] Children who are truly mentally retarded will have great difficulty in this area. Examples of adaptive behavior skills would include independent functioning (e.g., eating, dressing, toilet use), physical development (sensory and motor), economic activity (e.g., money and shopping skills), language development, number/time skills, prevocational/vocational activities, self-direction (e.g., initiative, perseverance, use of leisure time), responsibility, and so on. Depending on the degree of subaverage intellectual functioning and severity of maladaptive behavior skills, students with mental retardation will be classified as mild (formerly called "educable"), moderate (formerly "trainable"), or severe/profound in their condition.

Emotional/Behavior Disorders

Children with emotional/behavior disorders, along with those classified as learning disabled or mentally retarded represent a specific group of children referred to as *mildly disabled*.[23,24] The U.S. Department of Education[25] has indicated that approximately 75% of the total population of disabled students in this country have mild conditions of disability.

Emotional/behavior disorders, (now more commonly referred to as "behavior disorders") are the most difficult to diagnose and classify in children. Hallahan and Kauffman report that much subjectivity is presently involved in identifying these students since "no one has come up with an objective standard that is understandable and acceptable."[26] Nonetheless, it is generally agreed that behavior disordered students will exhibit behaviors that are *extremely different* (not just somewhat different), *chronic* (i.e., not short-lived), and *unacceptable* (when viewed in light of social or cultural expectations).

Emotionally/behaviorally disordered students generally have low-normal intelligence levels, yet show academic deficits in their school work (one or more years below their assigned grade level). In addition, their characteristic behaviors include hyperactivity, distractibility, impulsivity, overt aggression (e.g., arguing, cruelty, fighting, disobedience, threatening), covert antisocial acts (e.g., truancy, negativism, poor peer associations, destructiveness), anxiety-withdrawal (e.g., fearfulness, feelings of inferiority, oversensitivity), depression, and/or general unhappiness.[27,28]

In most Christian circles, people continue to grapple with the legitimacy of disabling conditions. Many simply don't believe that disabilities are real, despite the fact that there are clear examples of disabilities in Scripture.[29] However, based on Scriptural evidences of disabilities, our extensive study of research on the various forms of disability, and our personal experience teaching children with disabilities, we have no problem accepting the legitimacy of any of the disabilities discussed in this chapter except for emotional/behavior disorders. Our view is that many of the students identified in public schools as "behaviorally disordered" are simply not emotionally/behaviorally disabled at all. Rather they are suffering from what every human has since Adam, and that is a *spiritual disability*. Their actions and attitudes prior to demonstration of inappropriate behaviors are more reflective of intentional disobedience and defiance of authority, which are behaviors that emanate from unrighteous, sinful hearts and sin natures that have been allowed to run out of control by parents and school officials. We find it interesting that Kauffman[30] identifies research which has concluded that certain temperaments in children, if left unharnessed and unmanaged (i.e., undisciplined), could develop into so-called behavior disorders.

We do believe that there are some genuine cases of emotional/ behavior disorders in children, albeit *very few*. We have personally read evaluation reports of students who have biologically-based, chemical imbalances which produce extreme, chronic, and totally unacceptable behavior in Christian contexts. But these cases are rare. We believe that, in order to prove the legitimacy of a behavior disorder, the following additional requirements must be satisfied as part of a full, comprehensive evaluation of the child:

- Evidence of significantly low ratings on at least two different behavior rating scale instruments (see Chapter 5 on Testing and Evaluation);
- Verification of behavior problems through at least three classroom observations (randomly selected times) over an extended time period and in different settings (e.g., playing with others, during school work, etc.);
- Interviews with parents/teachers to determine whether the student's poor behavior is extreme, chronic, and unacceptable based on the Christian culture and expectations;
- Determination of whether the child's behavior is due to "noncompliance" (i.e., overt disobedience or rebellion) or "incompetence" (i.e., insufficient or no instruction in how to behave correctly) or long-term memory deficit;
- Evidence of a physiological, biological, biochemical, and/or neurological basis for the problem behaviors (which would require substantiation through a neurological examination— e.g., electroencephalogram [EEG], etc.).

Physical/Other Health Impairments

Although it represents only a very small proportion (about 5 in every 100) of the disabled population of school-age children, a myriad of conditions fall under the category of physical and other health impairments. Examples would include cancer, hemophilia, diabetes, sickle cell anemia, clubfeet, and even AIDS. By definition, physically impaired students are those whose physical limitations or health problems interfere with school attendance or learning to such an extent that special service, training, equipment, materials, or facilities are required. [and] whose *primary* characteristics are [not] visual or auditory impairments.[31]

It is important to note, however, that physically impaired students may have visual and/or hearing problems that are secondary to their primary physical problem(s). In addition, these students may also have "mental retardation, emotional disturbance, speech and language disorders, or special gifts or talents"[32] that coexist with their physically disabling condition.

Neurologically-based physical impairments would include such conditions as cerebral palsy, epilepsy (seizure disorders), spina bifida, poliomyelitis, and multiple sclerosis. There are also physical impairments of the *musculoskeletal* type, such as muscular dystrophy and arthritis. Other causes of physical impairment include *congenital malformations* (of the heart, hip, legs, arms, head, and/or face), *accidents* (e.g., burning, poisoning, bike/car mishaps), *child abuse* (e.g., physical, mental, sexual abuse), and *child neglect* (e.g., nutritional neglect).[33] Children are generally classified as physically impaired by medical doctors.

Attention Deficit Disorder

One of the newest recognized disabilities to date that would fall under the category of other health impairment is attention deficit hyperactivity disorder (the more common term is "attention deficit disorder" or ADD). Children with ADD may now receive special education under the classification of "other health impairment" if school officials determine that their condition is a "chronic or acute health problem that results in limited alertness, which adversely affects educational performance."[34] When the 3% to 5% of ADD students are factored in, the overall percentage of students with disabilities in this country has the potential to soar up to 15%.

ADD is *not* a form of "learning disability" or vice versa, but a distinct disabling condition in and of itself. Children classified as ADD must meet certain behavioral criteria. The American Psychiatric Association (APA) has specified 14 different behaviors that may characterize a student with ADD. They are as follows:

- Often fidgets with hands or feet or squirms in seat (in adolescents, may be limited to subjective feelings of restlessness);
- Has difficulty remaining seated when required to do so;
- Is easily distracted by extraneous stimuli;
- Has difficulty awaiting turn in games or group situations;
- Often blurts out answers to questions before they have been completed;
- Has difficulty following through on instructions from others (not due to oppositional behavior or failure of comprehension), e.g., fails to finish chores;
- Has difficulty sustaining attention in tasks or play activities;
- Often shifts from one uncompleted activity to another;
- Has difficulty playing quietly;
- Often talks excessively;
- Often interrupts or intrudes on others (e.g., butts into other children's games);
- Often does not seem to listen to what is being said to him or her;
- Often loses things necessary to tasks or activities at school or at home (e.g., toys, pencils, books, assignments);
- Often engages in physically dangerous activities without considering possible consequences (not for the purpose of thrill-seeking), e.g., runs into street without looking.[35]

Most people will recognize immediately that all children will exhibit some of these behaviors at one time or another in their lives. But the APA has stipulated that children with ADD will show at least eight of these behaviors, not just a couple, and will do them much more frequently than most children of the same ability. Moreover, the eight or more behaviors *must* have occurred for the first time before the child has reached seven years of age and must have existed for at least six months.

ADD students will generally have problems in one or more of these three areas: inattention, impulsivity, and hyperactivity. Not all ADD children exhibit behavior problems in all three areas, however. Some will show behavior problems predominately in inattention and impulsivity only. The effect of the ADD condition is the same in most students, though, regardless of the different combinations of behaviors. Their school work and performance in academics many times will take a plunge and their organizational skills and interactions with friends are less than desirable.[36] Like LD students, ADD students will have *normal intelligence* for the most part, which sets them apart from students who may have severe attentional problems that result from other disabilities such as mental retardation. At the time of this writing, the APA has developed a new listing of ADD behaviors along with a different set of criteria,[37] although it is still in draft form.

Hearing Impairments

Students who are deaf or hearing impaired can be born with the condition (congenital) or may acquire it sometime after birth (adventitious). One system of classifying these students hinges on the amount of hearing loss which is typically measured in decibels by an audiologist. Decibel units are a measure of intensity or loudness of sound. With the use of a pure tone audiometer, an audiologist will determine the student's threshold (beginning or onset) for hearing sound. Students with normal hearing should be able to hear sounds at 0 decibels (db). Those with a hearing loss will only be able to hear sounds at decibel levels of greater magnitude and are classified with varying levels of hearing loss as follows: 26-54 db (mild); 55-69 db (moderate); 70-89 (severe); and 90 db and above (profound).[38]

Another system of classification for students with hearing impairment is more educational in nature. School officials who will be providing special education for these children are more concerned with the extent to which hearing loss affects the development and use of language. Under this system, "deaf" students are those who cannot process language through their hearing sense, even with the use of hearing devices. Those who can successfully process language though hearing devices are considered "hearing impaired."[39]

The intellectual ability of hearing impaired students has been a point of considerable controversy among experts for some time now.[40] Since intelligence testing has traditionally relied upon intact hearing ability and spoken language processing skills, those with hearing impairment have tended to earn lower intelligence scores on these tests. It is now believed, however, that if these students are administered tests via manual communication (e.g., sign language), their intelligence scores would not fall in the retardation range.[41]

Visual Impairments

A visual impairment, like a hearing impairment, is a sensory disability and not a cognitive or academic form of disability, although both a visual and a hearing impairment can adversely affect a child's learning and achievement. Visual impairments can be defined from both a legal and an educational perspective.

The legal classification system is based on *visual acuity* (how clearly one can see) and *field of vision* (i.e., one's peripheral vision) skills. According to Hallahan and Kauffman, a legally blind person has "visual acuity of 20/200 or less in the better eye even with correction (e.g., eyeglasses) or has a field of vision so narrow that its widest diameter subtends an angular distance no greater than 20 degrees."[42] A person who is legally partially blind/ sighted will have a visual acuity between 20/70 and 20/200 in the better eye with corrective lenses. One should interpret a visual acuity level such as "20/70" to mean that the visually impaired student can see at 20 feet what a normally-sighted person can see at 70 feet.

The educational definition of visual impairment, as opposed to the legal definition, is based on the child's mode of reading instruction. If the child's vision is so impaired that he cannot read print and must use Braille or audiotapes/records in order to learn to read, then he is considered blind. Low vision students, on the other hand, are visually impaired students who can read print, but must have the print enlarged through magnification or large-print books (or copier enlargements).

Human nature as it is, some people may doubt the intellectual capabilities of visually impaired students. They surmise that if a student is not created perfectly whole then he cannot think, reason, and learn satisfactorily. But like students with hearing impairment, "there is no reason to believe that blindness results in lower intelligence."[43]

Giftedness

Giftedness is an exceptionality that is different from the other disabilities discussed earlier in that it is a *positive* condition that we want to foster in a child, not eliminate or eradicate. Gifted students do not have academic deficits that need remediation per se, rather they have an abundance of certain skills and talents that should be encouraged. Unlike students with learning disabilities, attention deficit disorders, or mental retardation, the gifted student's exceptionality is not preventing him from achieving or performing at acceptable levels. On the contrary, he comes into a typical learning situation many times having mastered in whole or in part already the skill or task that is being taught. Nonetheless, gifted children will still need a special education that is designed to meet their unique needs. For the most part, they will need either accelerated instruction and/or enrichment activities as a routine part of their school day.

Traditionally, the label of gifted and talented has been reserved for those students who scored unusually high on intelligence tests. This somewhat limited and narrow, single-criterion definition for giftedness has presented problems for educators through the years. Surely, our readers have known people who showed unusual brilliance intellectually and were considered gifted, but simply could not demonstrate or manifest their gift through some "remarkable or valued contribution to the human condition."[44] Yet there have been other students with only high average intelligence (and, hence, were not considered gifted) who nonetheless demonstrated their unusual talent by excelling in some performance/skill area (e.g., music, drama, athletics, etc.).

Renzulli, Reis, and Smith[45] have suggested a new definition for giftedness that requires that the child meet three criteria for classification, which are (1) high ability (includes an elevated intelligence level), (2) high creativity, and (3) high task commitment. Moreover, Renzulli and his colleagues hold that the individual is gifted only if he "applies [these three characteristics] to performance in a specific endeavor."[46] The specific performance areas are numerous and might include cartooning, poetry, costume design, architecture, cooking, agriculture, and many others. We must move away from the typical misconception that gifted students are only the "bookworms" in our classrooms. A truly gifted student can in fact be one whose area of talent and excellence falls outside the boundaries of paper-and-pencil tests or straight-A's on a report card.

[1]U.S. Department of Education (1992)
[2]J. Sutton, Wayne, Lanier, & Salars (1992)
[3]J. Sutton, Everett, & C. Sutton (1993)
[4]Hallahan & Kauffman (1991)
[5]U.S. Department of Education (1992)
[6]Wolf (1994)
[7]J. Sutton (1993)
[8]Beechick (1993), p. 45
[9]Clements (1966)
[10]Hallahan & Kauffman (1991)
[11]Lerner (1983)
[12]Hallahan & Kauffman (1991)
[13]Hallahan & Kauffman (1991)
[14]Hallahan & Kauffman (1991), p. 142
[15]*Federal Register,* December 19, 1977, p. 65083
[16]*Federal Register,* December 19, 1977, p. 65083
[17]U.S. Department of Education, 1992
[18]Hallahan & Kauffman (1991)
[19]Hallahan & Kauffman (1991)
[20]Patton, Bierne-Smith, & Payne (1990)
[21]Luckasson, Coulter, Polloway, Reiss, Schalock, Snell, Spitalnick, & Stark (1992)
[22]Lambert, Nihira, & Leland (1993), p. 2
[23]Houck & McMcKenzie (1988)
[24]Kelly & Vergason (1991)
[25]U.S. Department of Education (1986)
[26]Hallahan & Kauffman (1991), p. 174
[27]Hallahan & Kauffman (1991)
[28]Kauffman (1989)
[29]J. Sutton (1991)
[30]Kauffman (1989)
[31]Hallahan & Kauffman (1991), p. 344
[32]Hallahan & Kauffman (1991), p. 344
[33]Hallahan & Kauffman (1991)
[34]U.S. Department of Education (1991), p. 3
[35]APA (1987), p. 52-53
[36]J. Sutton (1994d)
[37]Task Force on DSM-IV (1993)

[38]Hallahan & Kauffman (1991)
[39]Brill, MacNeil, & Newman (1986)
[40]Hallahan & Kauffman (1991)
[41]Sullivan (1982)
[42]Hallahan & Kauffman (1991), p. 304
[43]Hallahan & Kauffman (1991), p. 302
[44]Hallahan & Kauffman (1991), p. 405
[45]Renzulli, Reis, & Smith (1981)
[46]Hallahan & Kauffman (1991), p. 406

3

ESSENTIAL TEACHING BELIEFS

For teaching in the home to be most effective, parents will need to establish a core set of teaching beliefs. Teaching beliefs are to a child's education like the foundation is to a building. It is interesting to note how meticulously careful contractors construct the foundation of a building, yet they may rush and be somewhat lax at times in finishing other aspects of the structure (e.g., the dry walling or painting). Rarely, though, will they be careless in the foundation of the building. Why is this? Given human nature and the depravity of man, contractors may be more concerned for the moment about meeting required building codes! But beyond this, we know that the foundation must be carefully constructed because the continued strength and longevity of the building in the years to come and its ability to withstand time and the environment depends largely on the stability of the foundation.

So it is with one's philosophy of teaching. A parent's core set of teaching beliefs and the values she embraces (i.e., philosophy) will directly affect every instructional decision she makes about and for her child, now and in the future. This would include such things as choice of curricula, materials, methods of teaching, and even expectations of success that a teacher would convey to the child along the way. In order for parents to teach struggling learners and others with disabilities properly and effectively, a Christian philosophy of teaching must be understood from the start.

But what does philosophy mean? Of the 11 definitions listed[1] for "philosophy," three have particular relevance for the teaching parent. Philosophy, as it relates to teaching, includes three essential elements: (a) fundamental beliefs; (b) motivating concepts and principles; and (c) values. In short, for the parent of a struggling learner, philosophy has to do with what she believes about teaching that child.

One of the basic requirements to teaching struggling learners effectively at home, as we shall discuss more fully in the chapters to come, is individualizing and tailor-making instruction for these children, which conventional educators typically refer to as "special education." It would be easy, then, for parents to adopt the public educators' philosophy of special education, and be done with it. But we agree with Vaughn,[2] who cautions that, in order to describe a *Christian* philosophy of special education, one must be careful not to "Christianize...secular special education philosophy."

What Bible-believing, Christian parents believe about their children who struggle with regard to who they are and how they should be taught runs counter to much of what public special educators believe about these children. In fact, the special education movement in America from the start reflected an inherently wrong motive, for it represented a self-centered, self-serving mission. Early proponents argued that students with disabilities had a "right" to an appropriate education in the public schools. Christian parents will recognize immediately that, as the Lord's people, none of us really have any "rights" per se. All we have and will ever be is granted to us by the grace and goodness of our God. Even the salvation we have is not a right, rather it is a gift and a privilege from a loving God (John 3:16).

While we agree that all struggling learners, particularly those with disabilities, should have an appropriate education that is designed to meet their unique needs, we disagree with the sometimes militant, "civil rights" approach that preceded the passage of federal laws in the 1970's which mandated special education in American public schools. Thus, we do not believe that we should offer to our readers a Christianized approach to secular special education. Instead, we believe that the system of teaching beliefs that should guide Christian parents who have struggling learners must stem directly from God's Holy, infallible Word.

Therefore, the five basic, Scriptural teaching beliefs and principles that follow are essential for parents of struggling learners to follow from the beginning if their home instruction is to be effective and successful in the long-run. There are other Bible truths and principles that we could share here, but the five that we have identified are the ones that are most applicable to teaching children with disabilities. Parents who have *non*disabled struggling learners with serious problems in learning, attention, and/or behavior problems should also consider these five principles carefully, for these Biblical truths are applicable to their home instruction, too.

These five teaching principles can be deceptively simple. At first glance, a parent may conclude that they are a bit elementary. Although this may be true to some degree, in a day and age where truth is constantly being attacked, challenged, and diluted by liberal unbelievers, it is critically important that we acknowledge and reaffirm these basic, godly teaching principles as the basis for teaching struggling learners and children with disabilities in the home.

Principle One

Students with disabilities have a sin nature and will sin. Unlike Rousseau, the great philosopher/teacher of centuries past who believed that all children were inherently good, God's Word is unmistakenly clear that all men (and students) are sinners. There is simply nothing good in man. One doesn't have to read too far into the Scripture to realize just how sinful man really is. In the first book of Genesis (3:1-6), God tells us that man fell into sin. We are told in Psalm 51:5 that man was born into sin. Numerous passages in the New Testament teach that mankind continues to inherit a sinful nature (Romans 3:9-12; Romans 5:12; I Cor. 15:21-22).

Accepting this principle as truth is not difficult for most Christian parents who have nondisabled children, particularly when they see their children in selfish moments. Some parents who have a child with a disability, though, may find it very hard to accept the fact that the child with all his limitations and afflictions also has a weakness with sin. Perhaps they reason that the disability in and of itself is enough for the child to bear, and that a loving, benevolent

God would not require the child to bear a sin nature, too. It would be very easy to excuse away a disabled child's sin nature, but to do so, again, would be a denial of the truth. There is no exception to Romans 3:23 that "ALL [with emphasis] have sinned and come short of the glory of God." All children, disabled and nondisabled alike, have a sin nature and will sin.

No doubt parents will come to a point where they have difficulty discerning whether a particular unacceptable behavior is emanating from the child's God-given disability or from his sin nature. Only the Lord will be able to provide the wisdom necessary to discern the difference when those times come. What is unfortunate is that some sincere and well-meaning, but ignorant people automatically assume that rebellion, laziness, character flaws and the like are the sole basis for *all* learning and/or behavior problems that children may have. Although this may in fact be true for many nondisabled children who misbehave and fail in their school work, we cannot accept this explanation for every learning and behavior problem of children who have documented forms of disability. Parents of disabled children must accept the fact that some troublesome behaviors are indeed a by product of the child's God-given disability, exercise reasonable patience and tolerance, and make every attempt to correct these behaviors with the Lord's help over time.

Principle Two

A student's disability is not necessarily a reflection of God's judgment on his or his parents' sin. There is a tendency many times in Christian circles to attribute automatically a person's misfortune to God's judgment on some prior sin that the person has committed. Someone suffers a heart attack or has terminal cancer, and the first thought that comes to some Christians' minds is that the person has been involved in some gross sin and that God is judging the sin through sickness. Some even believe this to be the reason why students have disabilities. Either the student himself or his parents are being judged by God for some sin one or both have committed.

The Lord Jesus refuted this line of thinking in His day, however. In John 9, we read the account of a blind man. The disciples, like many people today, had surmised that the man's blind condition was a reflection of God's hand of judgment for someone's sin, for they asked, "Master, who did sin, this man, or his parents, that he was born blind?" Christ immediately corrected them by saying, "Neither hath this man sinned, nor his parents: but that the works of God should be made manifest in him." We believe that God is simply glorified in His creation of children with disabilities.

We cannot infer from this passage, however, that Christ was teaching that absolutely no disabilities are ever the result of sin. God may in fact choose to disable a student in some way for continual, unconfessed sin. But whether He does or doesn't should not prevent us from providing the right kind of help for the student, whether it be educational or spiritual. After all, God does not withhold spiritual remediation from unrighteous, "spiritually disabled" mankind. Therefore, we should emulate our God, and our concern should not be on determining whether or not the child's disability is a result of God's hand of judgment, but to ensure that the disabled child receives instruction that meets his unique needs. If the individualized (special) education that we are providing the child is Bible-based and emphasizes spiritual truth, then all of the child's needs, spiritual and otherwise, will be sufficiently met.

We must get our thinking straight with regard to how we view children with disabilities. To look at them (or their parents) in a skeptical way as if they might have possibly committed some great sin and that they may be suffering God's judgment will surely taint all of our dealings and interactions with them. We give these children far too little credit in being able to "read" our true feelings and emotions with regard to how we view their disability, when in fact, they are very perceptive many times. Accepting students with disabilities as the unique creation of God that they are is the best position to take. The Psalmist wrote, "for we are fearfully and wonderfully made" (Ps. 139:14) and "His way is perfect" (Ps. 18:30). We agree with Behymer,[3] who has stated that "When God chooses to allow a disability to [exist and] remain, He is best glorified by our acceptance of the person as God made him."

Principle Three

Students with disabilities must learn Truth, accept the Lord Jesus as Savior, and gain spiritual understanding. It is the primary obligation of parents who have children with disabilities to teach Truth (II Tim. 2:2; Prov. 8:6-9). The fact that the child has a disability and may be viewed by the world as different does not change the fact that parents are bound and obligated to teach Truth. It matters not the type of disability that the child has or the severity of it. The home teacher's obligation is to teach Truth, and the disabled student must learn Truth.

What is Truth? The Scriptures indicate that the Word is Truth (Jn. 17:17), the Holy Spirit is Truth (Jn. 16:13), the fear of the Lord is Truth (Prov. 1:7), and the Lord Jesus Himself is Truth (Jn 14:6). There are many educational approaches to remediating a child's learning and behavior problems (and we will discuss these in later chapters), but there is only one way to correct a child's sin problem and that is through the Lord Jesus Christ, who is the Way, the Truth, and the Life. Our first and foremost spiritual obligation in teaching children with disabilities in the home is to see them accept the Lord Jesus as their personal Savior and be saved.

The teaching of truth must permeate everything that a parent would teach a disabled child in the home and must be reinforced continually, making home special education distinctively and thoroughly Christian. The methods the teacher employs should be ones that are capable of conveying truth. But methods are a means to an end, that end being the teaching and acceptance of truth, not an end in and of themselves. Not all methods used in the field of special education are a means of teaching truth. For example, various humanistic approaches such as reality therapy and life space interviewing,[4] which do not hold the student accountable for his behavior, have no place in a Christian program of home instruction.

Bringing children to a saving knowledge of Christ is not the culminating end of all spiritual teaching in the home school.

Parents must continue teaching Truth so that children with disabilities will gain spiritual understanding (Prov. 14:6; Prov. 18:1; Prov. 2:3-5). As part of their continued spiritual teaching, parents should help disabled children understand their uniqueness as God's own creation and how He made them with a purpose in mind. Children with disabilities desperately need to understand that they are not freaks or accidents of nature. They will need to learn fully of the great God who loves them supremely and unconditionally.

Principle Four

Students with disabilities must learn Christlikeness and acquire godliness of character. We believe that many parents often have the idea that we should place children with disabilities on a different educational agenda. That is, we should be teaching radically different things to disabled children since they show considerable differences at times (or even much of the time) from their nondisabled counterparts. This is simply not the case. Skill for skill, ability for ability, we believe that there are more likenesses and similarities between children with disabilities and those that are not disabled than there are differences. Therefore, we hold that teaching children with disabilities should not be that different at all from what we would normally teach nondisabled children.

Like nondisabled children, children with disabilities need to learn Christian character and how to live godly lives for the Lord. This is, in fact, the primary purpose of our teaching in the home. This main purpose differs from what public school educators perceive the main goal of education to be. Instead, they believe that getting children ready to make a contribution to this world, or teaching them how to earn money in order to pay bills, or helping them become literate are the most important reasons we are in the business of educating. Although none of these goals are inherently evil, these are secondary to the primary purpose of building Christian character in our children's lives.

We know that Christian character in a disabled child's life will be manifested through his inward relationship with God and his outward relationship with man. For example, in relation to God, it is important that disabled children, despite the limitations God has

allowed, learn to glorify God in all that they do and accomplish
(I Cor. 10:31), love the Lord with all their hearts (Deut. 6:5; Matt.
22:37), obey the Lord right away and at all times (II Cor. 10:5),
recognize that they can only be made complete in Him (II Tim.
3:17), and refrain from self-service and self-centeredness (Phil.
2:3-5). In relation to man, we should teach children with disabilities to obey their parents (Eph. 6:1), to love one another (Matt.
22:39), to refrain from offending others (I Cor. 10:32; II Cor. 6:3),
and to do good unto all men (Gal. 6:10).

Principle Five

*Students with disabilities must recognize their God-given
abilities and place of service to the Lord.* We must bring children
with disabilities to the point in their spiritual lives that they recognize that they are indeed bought with a price, that price being the
life blood of the Lord Jesus Himself. We are not our own; we are
all bought with a price (Rom. 12:1-2; I Cor. 6:20). The purchase of
our lives by the Lord Jesus' death means that we are to serve Him
for the remainder of our days on this earth in whatever field of
service that He calls us, and it should be done lovingly and not
begrudgingly.

Children, disabled and nondisabled alike, will need to learn
that God has a purpose for each and every person's life. Parents
must teach continually two very important truths here. One is that
"Every child has everything he needs in order to do God's will for
his life."[5] We must not think that just because a child has a *disability* that he does not have some *abilities* with which to serve God.
On the contrary, we know that "every man hath received the gift"
(I Peter 4:10). As we have noted with other verses, this passage
does *not* exclude those with disabilities. Each one has a gift with
which to serve God and to minister to others. The Lord will not
call all to preach or teach. He won't call all to be engineers and
lawyers. Whatever the calling or the gift, though, God will equip
and empower each person to serve as He wills.

A second related truth is that "For a Christian, life is not divided into the secular and the sacred. To him all ground is holy
ground ..."[6] No one calling is more important in the Lord's sight
than another calling, and students with disabilities must recognize

that their calling in life from God will be sacred, too. The service they render to the Lord will be just as unique, just as needed, and will produce a savor that is just as sweet as the services rendered by those nondisabled individuals whom the Lord calls. The place of service in which the Lord places a disabled individual may not be as prominent as that of other nondisabled people, but it is still an important place of service nonetheless. Behymer aptly writes:

> Unfortunately, earthly ideas of success still dominate our thinking. We often establish a person's value by how much he earns, owns, or contributes to society. For example, the status of a physician is generally thought of as higher than that of a street sweeper. These attitudes could not be farther from the truth shown in God's Word....It is not up to us to decide whether or not a disabled person's contribution in life is worth something....We are to look at disabled people as God does and do our best to help each one reach the full potential that God has given him.[7]

In sum, we encourage our readers to make a commitment before God to adhere to the following five basic Bible principles that we have presented in this chapter and to make them an integral part of their teaching philosophy:

- Students with disabilities have a sin nature and will sin;
- A student's disability is not necessarily a reflection of God's judgment on his or his parents' sin;
- Students with disabilities must learn Truth, accept the Lord Jesus as Savior, and gain spiritual understanding;
- Students with disabilities must learn Christlikeness and acquire godliness of character; and
- Students with disabilities must recognize their God-given abilities and place of service to the Lord.

---

[1] *American Heritage Dictionary* (1985)
[2] Vaughn (1993), p. 21
[3] Behymer (1993), p. 289
[4] Heuchert & Long (1980)
[5] Vaughn (1993), p. 22
[6] Jones (no date), p. 5
[7] Behymer (1993), p. 290

SCRIPTURAL MODEL FOR TEACHING

The Scriptures are replete with examples of how God used various methods and simple, everyday objects to teach His people. He used a *tree* to teach Adam and Eve in the Garden of Eden about the eternal consequences of disobedience (Gen. 3:17). He used a *rainbow* to teach the small remnant of people that survived with Noah that He would never again use a universal flood to destroy the earth (Gen. 9:13-15). He used the *tabernacle* in the Old Testament to teach of the Savior, the Lord Jesus, to come (Heb. 9:11). When the scribes and Pharisees brought the adulteress before the Lord Jesus in an effort to tempt and accuse Him, Christ's method of pronouncing judgment on these men included stooping down and *writing on the ground* (Jn. 8:6).

We see the ultimate of teaching methods demonstrated by God Himself in the plan of salvation He offers to disobedient man. For those who know the Lord Jesus as personal Savior, the specific elements of God's method of salvation are precious. God loved us so much that He sent His only begotten Son, Christ Jesus, from the regal glories of heaven to earth so that He would die and intercede for pitiful, sinful men (Jn. 3:16). The Lord Jesus humbled Himself, took on the form of a servant and the likeness of a man, and gave up His life on a cruel, rugged cross to pay sin's price for all men and women, past, present, and future (Phil. 2:6-8). God's method of salvation does not end here, for the Scriptures tell us that God raised Him (Christ) from the dead (Acts 2:32), and He lives today and forevermore as the Mediator between God and men (I Tim. 2:5).

Scriptural Basis for the Model

It is within this context of salvation, relayed in two specific accounts of Christ's ministry, that we discover a key to how parents should meet the needs of struggling learners. Two separate passages of Scripture, both having to do with individuals who had disabilities—one with *blindness* (John 9:1-7), the other with *palsy*, a physically disabling condition (Mark 2:1-5,10-12)—provide the basis for a model of instruction that parents of struggling learners can implement in the home. Although Christ had other encounters with disabled persons (see Figure 4.1), we believe these two accounts provide a clear picture of how He taught them.

In both of these accounts, Christ, the Master Teacher, was involved in teaching and transforming the spiritual and physical lives of individuals with disabilities. Consider first the account of the blind man in John 9:1-7:

> *And as Jesus passed by, he saw a man which was blind from his birth. And his disciples asked him, saying, Master, who did sin, this man or his parents, that he was born blind? Jesus answered, Neither hath this man sinned, nor his parents: but that the works of God should be made manifest in him. I must work the works of him that sent me, while it is day: the night cometh, when no man can work. As long as I am in the world, I am the light of the world. When he had thus spoken he spat on the ground, and made clay of the spittle, and he anointed the eyes of the blind man with the clay. And said unto him, Go, wash in the pool of Siloam, (which is by interpretation, Sent.) He went his way, therefore, and washed, and came seeing.*

The second passage relaying the palsied man's experience with Christ is found in Mark 2:1-5, 10-12: It reads as follows:

> *And again he [Christ] entered into Capernaum, after some days, and it was noised that he was in the house. And straightway many were gathered together, insomuch that there was no room to receive them, no, not so much as about the door: and he preached the word unto them. And they come unto him, bringing one sick of the palsy, which was borne of four, And when they could not come nigh unto*

him for the press, they uncovered the roof where he was: and when they had broken it up, they let down the bed wherein the sick of the palsy lay. When Jesus saw their faith, He said unto the sick of the palsy, Son, thy sins be forgiven thee. [verses 10-12] But that ye may know that the Son of man hath power on earth to forgive sins, (he saith to the sick of the palsy), I say unto thee, Arise, and take up thy bed, and go thy way into thine house. And immediately he arose, took up the bed, and went forth before them all.

Figure 4.1

Christ's Encounters with Disabled Persons

Disability	Reference(s)
Blindness (VI)	Matt. 9:27-31; Matt. 20:29-34; Mk. 8:22-26; Mk. 10:46-52; Lk. 18:35-43; Jn. 9:1-7, 35-38
Blindness/Lame (VI/PI)	Mt. 14:21
Deafness/Speech (HI/CD)	Mk. 7:32-37
Dropsy (PI)	Lk. 14:1-6
Epilepsy (PI)	Matt. 17:14-21; Mk. 9:17-27; Lk. 9:37-42
Infirmity (PI)	Lk. 13:10-17; Jn. 4:1-16
Lame/Blind/Dumb/Maimed (MD)	Matt. 16:30-31
Leprosy (PI)	Matt. 8:1-4; Mk. 1:40-45; Lk. 5:12-16; Lk. 17:11-19
Palsy (PI)	Matt. 8:5-13; Matt. 9:1-8; Mk. 2:1-12; Lk. 5:18-26; Lk. 7:1-10
Withered Hand (PI)	Matt. 12:9-13; Mk. 3:1-5; Lk. 6:6-11

Legend: CD=Communication Disorder; HI=Hearing Impairment; MD=Multiple Disabilities; PI=Physical Impairment; VI=Visual Impairment.

Elements of the Teaching Model

Careful examination of both of these passages allow us to make several observations on how the Lord provided for the needs of persons with disabilities. We can extract three elements from His teaching that should comprise the home model for teaching struggling learners, which are: (1) one-on-one instruction; (2) methods tailored to the needs of the individual; and (3) alternative forms of assessment.

One-on-One Instruction

Foremost in Christ's dealings with these two men with disabilities was how He dealt with them *individually*, that is, *one-on-one*. He verbally interacted with them in an individual way. His chosen treatment was delivered individually. For both of these men, Christ performed two miracles in their lives—He saved them from their sins and He made their bodies whole again. God still deals with us today as individuals, does He not? He still saves us as individuals, forgives us individually of our sins, and meets individual needs that we have.

Herein lies the first element of a model for teaching students with disabilities and struggling learners in the home. We know these children will need one-on-one attention and instruction for the most part. It matters not what disabling condition they have. If the disability has an adverse effect on the child's ability to learn and achieve, then the child in all likelihood will need some degree of individualized instruction. Interestingly, individualized instruction is at the very heart of what special education programming was intended to be in our public schools.[1,2] Moreover, individualized instruction in the form of individualized educational plans (IEP) is mandated by federal law (Public Laws 94-142 and 101-476) for all children enrolled in public school special education programs.

Unfortunately, individualized instruction does not necessarily mean that children in conventional school special education programs will be getting one-on-one instruction. In fact, in most public schools, individualized instruction for many children with disabilities is delivered in small group settings. Teacher-student ratios in special education classrooms at these schools will vary based on state mandated guidelines. We know one thing for sure, though. The teacher-student ratio in most public school special education classrooms will not be 1:1 (i.e., one teacher to one student). Even recommendations from scholars in the field go well beyond a 1:1 teacher-student ratio. For example, Zacherman[3] recommends a 1:5 ratio, Reger[4] says it should be 1:3 or 1:4, and Zimmerman[5] believes that some children with disabilities can survive quite nicely in larger groups where the student-teacher ratio is between 1:7 and 1:10.

In addition to high teacher-student ratios per class hour, the total number of students many public school special education teachers have to serve per day is horrendously high. For example, in Virginia public schools, some resource special education teachers have to serve as many as 24 different children with disabilities over the course of a school day.[6] So, both high teacher-student ratios per class hour and high student case loads per day are detriments to ensuring ideal individualized instruction for children with disabilities in public schools.

Clearly, parents have the advantage over conventional classroom teachers in this area of providing one-on-one instruction. We agree with Somerville[7] that there is no better or more convenient educational setting than the home to provide individualized, one-on-one instruction. White,[8] citing the benefits of a home instructional setting for ADD students, states that, "the child does not have to contend with the noise and distractions of 20 other students." In a first study of its kind to determine the effectiveness of home instruction with learning disabled students, Duvall[9] concluded that parents, "provided powerful instructional environments at home that...[made] significant improvements in [LD students'] basic skills." He cited low student numbers in home schools as an integral part of these students' success.

Methods Tailored to Needs

When we analyze the two Scripture passages further, we find that more was done instructionally for these two disabled men. In addition to one-on-one instruction, a second provision made for them was the application of a special, non-conventional teaching method that was tailored to meet their individual needs. Tailored teaching methods are the second element of a proper home instruction program for struggling learners.

For the blind man, Christ "made clay of the spittle, and He anointed the eyes of the blind man with the clay." For the palsied man, the men "uncovered the roof where [Christ] was...and they let down the bed" of the palsied man so Christ could deal with him. In both cases, the program or method used in treating the limitations of these two men, both spiritually and physically, was tailor-made to meet their unique needs and was altered from the usual.

One of the problems that conventional school special education teachers face daily is finding the necessary time to develop individualized programs, methods, and instructional modifications that will work best for each of their students. This task is almost insurmountable when we recognize how many students each teacher must serve, as we have discussed in earlier paragraphs. Given that conventional school special education teachers have the potential to serve as many as 20 to 25 different children per day, it is very difficult, although not impossible, to develop tailor-made instructional programs for this many children.

Again, we believe that the teaching parent has the advantage over conventional educators here. The typical family will probably have no more than one or two children with bona fide disabilities (although it is possible for some families to have several struggling learners); hence, there is ample time for parents to identify the characteristics and needs of the child and develop methods and programs that are appropriate for him/her.

Alternative Forms of Assessment

There was a third and final provision made for the blind man and the palsied man by the Lord Jesus. Please note that both the mode of and response to assessment (i.e., how Christ evaluated what He had taught the two men) was uniquely different from the usual, yet the assessment in each case corresponded to the characteristic difficulties that accompanied each man's disability. Thus, the third and final element to a proper model of home instruction for struggling learners is developing alternative forms of testing/ assessment for the child.

For the blind man, Christ instructed him to "Go...[and]...wash in the pool of Siloam." It was upon obedience to this action that the blind man "went his way, therefore, washed, and came seeing." The evaluation mode was a pool of water. The evaluation response was washing. For the palsied man, Christ instructed him to "Arise, and take up [his] bed, and go [his] way into [his] house," upon which the man "immediately...arose, took up the bed, and went forth before them all." The evaluation mode here was the bed. The evaluation response was taking up the bed and walking.

Parents who choose to teach their disabled children at home may also need to develop alternative assessment/evaluation modes and responses that are tailor-made to the needs of their children. Once more, we believe the teaching parent has the edge over public and/or private special educators in doing this. In all likelihood, home teachers may have more time and more flexible schedules to provide and administer alternative evaluation procedures.

Justification for the Model

Based on Christ's example to us, then, parents of struggling learners will need to provide one-on-one instruction, tailor-made programs and methods, and alternative forms of evaluation for their children. Since this model of special education is based on God's Word, it really needs no justification. Interestingly, we have had some to suggest to us that the one-on-one element of this teaching model, which naturally occurs in home education, is perhaps all that is necessary in meeting the unique needs of students with disabilities. Clearly, if we are to emulate Christ's example, much more has to be done if we are to teach children who struggle and those who may be disabled in our homes effectively.

Our view is that a parent who makes use of only the one-on-one instruction format is much like a soldier in warfare who is given a weapon to use in battle, but with no instructions or qualifications on how to use the weapon. Without a strategy or plan on when and how to engage the weapon properly in battle, the soldier's approach will probably be random and arbitrary. With no carefully thought-out plan, there is no guarantee that the mission for the battle will ever be accomplished, shy of a chance happening.

So it is with teaching struggling learners in the home. It is good to provide the one-on-one instruction and attention that they will need. But simply placing a struggling learner, particularly one with a disability, on a standard curriculum of study with only one-on-one assistance is in essence doing nothing more for him than we would naturally do for a child who does not struggle. One clear conclusion that we can draw from Christ's example to us is that He went above and beyond the way He would have typically taught a mass of people and accommodated for the unique needs of the blind and palsied man. We believe parents must do the same for struggling learners.

The Lord Jesus' approach was individualized, carefully thought-out, tailor-made, and systematic. A parent's instructional dealings with children who struggle or have disabilities in the home should be the same. If parents ever hope to remediate and eradicate the significant learning deficits in these children, one-on-one instruction must be supplemented with carefully planned, individualized, tailor-made programs and methods along with alternative evaluation procedures that are designed to meet their unique needs.

Of the three elements in the model, parents will probably have the most difficulty with the latter two—developing tailor-made teaching methods and choosing alternative assessment procedures. Chapters 8-12 provide parents with practical ideas and information in these two areas.

---

[1]Hallahan & Kauffman (1991)
[2]C. Mercer & A. Mercer (1993)
[3]Zacherman (1992)
[4]Reger (1973)
[5]Zimmerman (1982)
[6]J. Sutton (1989)
[7]Somerville (1994)
[8]White (1994), p. 46
[9]Duvall (1994), p. 11

TESTING AND EVALUATION

N ot all experiences in our lives are easy and enjoyable. There will be hard and difficult times that we all will have to endure as we grow and mature. Times of testing are one example. Many people bristle at the very mention of testing. Moreover, the idea of testing brings to mind unpleasant thoughts for many parents, for parents, like students, have been subjected to the demands and rigors of testing at one time or another in their lives. Testing nonetheless has played a critical role in the education of children throughout the ages.

Unfortunately, testing in education is typically viewed as a final measure of a child's learning *after* instruction has taken place. But for teaching struggling learners, testing and evaluation can play a much more powerful role. It can be used as a *beginning* step in planning effective instruction. But beyond learning about how it can be used instructionally, we believe there may be a more compelling reason why parents, particularly those who have struggling learners, should learn about testing and evaluation.

During our visits at various state and national home school conventions for speaking engagements over the last several years, we have become acquainted with scores of parents who expressed dissatisfaction with testing services they had received from professional examiners. Many admitted that, because they had no understanding of even the basic essentials of testing and evaluation, they had unintentionally contracted for testing that, in the long-run, produced little more than a technical report with fancy test scores and professional jargon. Simply put, individual testing for strug-gling learners is not only complex, but it is extremely expensive, with fees ranging generally from a few hundred to a thousand dollars or more. Thus, we believe parents would be in a better position to make wiser, more sound decisions in this area if they are knowledgeable about the basics of testing and evaluation.

The remainder of this chapter, then, will be devoted to the following topics related to testing struggling learners: (a) reasons for testing; (b) specific types of tests; (c) qualifications of examiners; and (d) how often testing should be conducted.

Reasons for Testing

We are not suggesting the need for testing just to make life more difficult (or financially burdensome) for parents and the struggling learner or just to be in keeping with what conventional educators are doing. On the contrary, if testing is understood properly and the findings implemented correctly in the home, it should make instruction much easier to plan and evaluate in the long run. Testing and evaluation should be done for struggling learners for four primary reasons: (1) identifying/verifying a disability; (2) determining current achievement (functioning) level; (3) diagnosing skill strengths/weaknesses; and (4) documenting progress.

Identifying/Verifying a Disability

Virtually all children will show some difficulties in learning, attention, and/or behavior throughout their grade school years. For example, it would not be unusual for a parent to observe a younger child (or even an older student!) daydreaming several times during the course of one school week. But with a small segment of the school-age population, difficulties in learning, attention, and/or behavior can be more frequent and persistent in the child's life. Not only do these difficulties remain across time, but they may even worsen as the child matures physically. Consider the following letter we received some time ago from one home educating mother:

> I really feel at the end of my rope with my son some-times. He's a wonderful, loving, caring boy, but at times I

just don't know what I am doing wrong. It has only lately occurred to me that he may have a learning disability. He has always out-performed his sister scholastically (and she's two years his senior). Some of the things that he has already learned I have never taught him. He has just been able to pick it up on his own (e.g., reading, relationships of math facts to one another, etc.).

But when I think of the lengths I have had to go to extract that information from him...the constant prodding (and I mean constant!) to complete the next assigned task, urging him to think about what he's doing...it simply dazzles me. I can't explain any other way how a child can remember exact details from events that occurred when he turned two, yet he cannot remember which direction the silverware drawer is when he is setting the table.

No discipline or reward system, or any other method I have tried (nor my husband) seems to help. Just recently, we spent hours doing one load of laundry. Actually he spent hours trying to do it, and I spent hours reminding, correcting, setting timers, disciplining, and generally just being frustrated with him. I've always taken this as something that is "normal," a typical behavior for a boy (his sisters never did things like this!). I've even thought that it could be a discipline problem with him but one that he would grow out of one day. But IT'S NOT GOING AWAY....So often I have wondered if I have failed him in some way because of the way I am (or am not) teaching him.

No doubt this mother was observing learning and behavior problems that were beyond what typical children experience. But how can a parent know if a child's behavior is *extremely different* from that of typical children? One way would be for parents to conduct their own informal home test. Suppose, for example, that a parent decides to observe and record her son's inattention over the course of four to six weeks and concludes that he is off-task and inattentive approximately eight times per hour. The parent further notes that the child did not appear to be intentionally not paying attention. Based on this small amount of informal, observational data, the parent should rightfully conclude that such severe inattention may be beyond what we might expect of a typical child and that such behavior could be indicative of an attention deficit disorder or other disability (See Chapter 2).

Only through formal testing and evaluation, though, can parents know for sure whether a child's observed learning, attention, and/or behavior problems are rooted in some form of a disability. Identifying a child's disability for instructional purposes can be likened unto diagnosing a physical illness that one might have. Suppose that your child has been suffering from stomach pains for several days. He has great difficulty keeping his food down. He looks increasingly pale and weak. He is sluggish in his play and work and tells you that he would rather lie in bed and rest than go out and play. You observe that these symptoms persist for several days in succession.

Few loving, caring parents would leave such a child to himself, hoping and praying that he will simply "shake off" these serious, potentially life-threatening symptoms. Let's face it. Most parents would yield to the expertise and counsel of medical personnel to examine the child thoroughly and would anxiously await a diagnosis of the problem. Moreover, most would proceed quickly to secure whatever medical assistance is necessary to bring the child back to full health.

Should parents do any less when their child shows signs of diminished performance in learning, attention, and/or behavior? Should they ignore children who are "suffering" in their school performance, not able to excel in their school work, failing to master the skills they are being taught in their educational programs? Should parents overlook it when children grow "pale and weak" in their enthusiasm and motivation for learning and when they are "sluggish" at improving in their studies and actions for prolonged periods of time? When children are able to do well in many other activities of their lives, but just can't seem to perform academically and behaviorally up to par, should parents pretend that such symptoms will not have an adverse effect on the child's academic success and/or self-concept in the long run?

Clearly, parents should not ignore persistent educational and behavioral problems in their children. Just as diagnosis and cure of medical problems are vital to the continuing good health and physical development of a child, so it is critically important that a child's serious learning/behavioral limitation (typically referred to as a "disability") be identified and remediated as early as possible.[1] The sooner we can pinpoint and define the specific disability that may be preventing a child from learning and behaving successfully, the sooner a tailor-made home special education program can be developed to meet his unique needs.

Testing for the purpose of identifying a child's disability is typically called a *psychological* or *psychoeducational evaluation.* Vergason defines an *evaluation* as "an appraisal or estimation of certain specific characteristics, such as intelligence, personality, or physical aspects of an individual."[2] In essence, an examiner will administer a set of different one-on-one tests that measure the child's intelligence, achievement, perceptual-motor skills, adaptive behavior skills, speech/language skills, behavior, attention skills, and so on (we discuss these different types of tests in the paragraphs to follow). The examiner will also collect other informal data on the child (e.g., parent observations/evaluations of child's school performance, samples of school work, medical records, other background information, etc).

Once all formal and informal data on the child have been collected, the examiner will conduct an in-depth analysis and provide a written report of findings and recommendations to the parent. A proper evaluation report should provide the following information about the child:

- Background information (birth process, medical history, etc.);
- Observations of behavior during testing;
- List of specific tests administered;
- Actual test scores (e.g., percentile ranks);
- Interpretation of test scores;
- A firm, clear, substantiated decision by the examiner regarding the presence or absence of a disability;
- Extent of special education programming needed ; and
- Some instructional recommendations.

The primary purpose of this type of testing, then, is to identify and/or verify the presence of a disability in the child, *not* to provide extensive diagnostic and instructional recommendations on how a home program should be tailored for the child. Therefore, parents should come away from the evaluation with a complete understanding of whether or not their child has a disability and the specific nature of it. With these test results, parents will know better how to set *reasonable expectations* for their child. Probably one of the most important benefits from psychoeducational testing is that parents will no longer feel personally responsible for the child's lack of success. If test results indicate a disability of some sort, then parents must accept the fact that God may be pleased for the child to have a limitation (see Chapter 2 and our discussion of Principle 2).

Determining Current Achievement Level

As we have stated earlier, parents need to develop tailor-made programs of instruction for struggling learners. We recommend that the program include two major strands of teaching: (1) remediation instruction—so that learning gaps can be closed; and (2) regular instruction that follows the typical scope and sequence of skills expected of students at a particular grade/age. Children with disabilities will not be able to achieve at optimum levels and progress educationally if they receive only regular instruction. The remediation strand of teaching will be critical, but it is no more important than the regular curriculum teaching strand, and vice versa. Both forms of instruction are essential for children with disabilities (Please refer to Chapter 8 for a more comprehensive discussion of these two strands of teaching).

To increase their success in regular instruction, children with disabilities should be studying from educational materials (which may include textbooks, workbooks, etc.) that are at their *functioning* or *instructional* level, rather than at a *frustrational* level of learning.[3] Many times we find these children studying from material that is beyond their current level of skill functioning. The end result is a frustrated child, whose overall school performance is less than satisfactory, sometimes failure. We illustrate the difference in levels of learning with the following example.

David has a learning disability in a conventional school setting, and he is presently placed in or assigned to fifth grade (i.e., he has completed kindergarten through fourth grades). Because of David's accompanying learning problems, he is not performing, functioning, or achieving at fifth grade level in most of his subjects. On the contrary, David, like many other children with mild forms of disability, is functioning at a grade level that is several grade levels below his current grade assignment. Having him learn from grade level curricula that is at his fifth grade placement will most likely be a frustrational learning experience for him. On the other hand, placing him on grade level materials that are at his current achievement level will allow him to move forward at a more successful, less frustrational pace.

Herein we see the second reason why testing and evaluation is so important for children with disabilities. We must use formal testing and evaluation to determine their present level of functioning or achievement. Specifically, the scores from the one-on-one achievement tests administered by the examiner during the psychoeducational evaluation will serve as a guideline for placement of the student on an appropriate standard curricula. We continue our scenario of David and illustrate.

Suppose David earned a grade equivalent (G.E.) score of 2.8 on the reading decoding (pronunciation) subtest and a 3.2 on the reading comprehension subtest on a one-on-one administered achievement test. Grade equivalent scores, like age equivalent scores, compare the individual child's performance to that of a large, representative sample of students across the country who were involved in the field-testing of the achievement test. Thus, we interpret David's score on the reading decoding subtest to mean that his performance is comparable to that of average students in the norm sample who were placed at the eighth month of their second grade year in school (i.e., G.E. of 2.8). In like manner, we interpret David's score on the reading comprehension to mean that his performance is comparable to that of average students in the norm sample who were placed at the second month of their third grade year (i.e., G.E. of 3.2). Based on these scores, the third grade level would serve as a good estimate of David's functioning or instructional level in reading. His parents should, therefore, choose a regular curricula in reading that reflects a third grade level, even though his actual grade placement is fifth grade.

Diagnosing Skill Strengths/Weaknesses

A second form of testing, sometimes referred to as "diagnostic" or "skill-based" evaluations, will generally follow the psychoeducational evaluation of a child. A diagnostic evaluation will include a number of one-on-one administered diagnostic tests that are designed to provide an in-depth assessment of the child's strengths and weaknesses in specific academic skill areas. Findings from a diagnostic evaluation will subsequently be used as a basis for planning remediation instruction in a tailor-made home education program.

Here is how diagnostic testing works. If a student has been found to have a learning disability in reading decoding skills, a diagnostic evaluation would pinpoint the specific type(s) of reading decoding skill problems the child possesses, which may include deficiencies in certain short or long vowel sounds, digraphs, beginning consonant sounds, or phonetic irregularities, etc. Similarly, if a student is found to have significant weaknesses in mathematics, a diagnostic evaluation would determine whether he is having problems in basic computation/operational math (e.g., adding and subtracting), geometric principles, fraction concepts, measurement skills, etc.

Diagnostic testing differs markedly from psychological or psychoeducational testing. The latter type of testing for the most part will produce only quantitative scores of the child's performance, for example, grade equivalent scores (3.4—third grade, fourth month), age equivalent scores (9-5—nine years, 5 months), standard scores (107—where the mean score is 100), and percentile ranks (58th—which means the child performed equal to or better than 58% of the norm sample). Hence, the primary purpose of psychoeducational testing is to compare a child's ability and performance with that of his age-peers, a comparison group, or a norm sample. Very little instructional information about the child's mastery of *specific* academic skills can be gleaned from psychoeducational testing, although parents do get a good idea of the child's abilities to learn.

Diagnostic tests, on the other hand, will measure a child's skill attainment against a standard body of skills in which he should be able to demonstrate mastery at a particular point in his life. The only resulting "number-type" score will be a simple count or percentage of how many skills he actually knows of the total number of skills he *should* know. In short, a properly administered diagnostic skill evaluation will produce a list of academic skills and subskills that the child has mastered and, more important, those in which he has not yet shown proficiency or mastery. The list of skills in which the child has not shown mastery can provide the home teacher with specific direction in *what* to teach the child during his remedial instruction time (see Chapter 8 for teaching techniques and methods on *how* parents can teach these skills).

By way of illustration, we have listed in Figure 5.1 the specific capitalization skills in which a student in third grade and a student in ninth grade would be expected to show mastery (as taken from the *BRIGANCE Diagnostic Comprehensive Inventory of Basic Skills*[4]). The number of specific academic skills in which a child should be expected to show mastery will vary based on the child's grade level. A student in the lower elementary grades (in this case, third grade) would not be expected to master as many academic subskills as a student in the upper grades (in this case, ninth grade). Findings from a diagnostic evaluation should subsequently be used as a basis for planning remediation activities in the child's tailor-made home program.

Documenting Progress

Parents, like teachers in conventional schools, will want to know whether their children are achieving as they should. One way of documenting child progress is through daily informal measures, which would include scores from independent school work, tests, projects, and the like. We will address how students with disabilities should be evaluated on an informal, daily basis in Chapter 11.

For students with disabilities, a more formal way of documenting progress would be through *one-on-one* administered achieve-

Figure 5.1

Expected Mastery for Capitalization Skills

Third Grade   Ninth Grade*

Third Grade	Ninth Grade*
• First word in sentence	• Bodies of water and landforms
• Pronoun "I"	• Special groups of people
• Names of people	• First word in direct quotation
• Days of the week	• Continents
• Special days/holidays	• Titles of books/stories/magazines
• Months of the year	• Business firms, brand names
• Streets and roadways	• Government groups
• Cities	• Proper adjectives
• States	• Historical events and periods
• Countries	• Religions and nationalities
• Titles of people	• Directions as regions
• Initials	• Ships, trains, and planes

*Ninth grade students learn these capitalization skills in addition to those expected of third graders.

ment tests or diagnostic tests (please note the following section for a more detailed description of these forms of testing). Generally, individually administered achievement tests will only need to be administered once a year, preferably near the end of the school year, between the months of April and June. Parents would then compare the child's current achievement test scores with scores earned on the same or similar test administered the prior year. The scores provided in Figure 5.2 below are achievement scores from a learning disabled student (seventh grade, age 12 years, 6 months) who was tested in 1992 and 1993, using selected subtests from the *Woodcock-Johnson Psycho-Educational Battery- Tests of Achievement.*[5] Sometimes the one-on-one standardized achievement test scores do not adequately show the amount of academic growth and progress that a child has made. In short, these types of tests and resulting scores do not always do justice in describing the successful learning of a child who has undergone special education pro-

Figure 5.2
Achievement Scores for an LD Student

Academic Skill	Age Equivalent		Grade Equivalent		Percentile Rank	
	1992	1993	1992	1993	1992	1993
Letter-Word Identification	8-10	11-7	3.6	6.2	16	39
Passage Comprehension	10-10	13-8	5.6	8.3	42	65
Mathematics Calculation	10-4	11-3	5.0	5.9	22	27

gramming for a year. For this reason, diagnostic test results may be more preferable. As we mentioned earlier, diagnostic tests will not generally produce the full array of standardized scores as the norm-referenced achievement tests do. But diagnostic tests can show in a more vivid way the progress that a child has made.

We illustrate our point by reexamining the learning disabled student's achievement scores in mathematics calculation. A comparison of the child's age equivalent, grade equivalent, and particularly her percentile rank scores do not reveal very much progress beyond normal development after one year. But consider the diagnostic mathematics scores from this same learning disabled student in the area of mathematics in Figure 5.3 (please note that the fractions in each column below represent the number of questions answered correctly of the total possible from the *KeyMath Revised: A Diagnostic Inventory of Essential Mathematics.*[6]

It may well be that the teaching parent desires to use both standardized, one-on-one achievement tests and diagnostic tests in documenting their child's yearly progress. Both types of test results when combined will provide a more complete and detailed picture of progress. Given that academic progress may come more slowly for students with disabilities, parents may find it more beneficial and encouraging to have both types of testing done periodically.

Specific Types of Tests

Formal tests for students with disabilities fall into three main categories: (1) psychological or psychoeducational tests;

(2) diagnostic skill tests; and (3) progress/achievement tests. These types of tests must be administered individually, one-on-one, by a professional examiner. Two other types of tests—screening tests

Figure 5.3

Diagnostic Mathematics Scores for an LD Student

Mathematics Skill	1992	1993	Percent Change
Numeration	14/21	17/21	+14.3%
Fractions	5/8	5/8	0%
Geometry/Symbols	17/18	17/18	0%
Addition	13/14	11/14	-14.3%
Subtraction	8/11	10/11	+18.2%
Multiplication	5/10	9/10	+40.0%
Division	4/8	6/8	+25.0%
Mental Computation	4/10	6/10	+25.0%
Numerical Reasoning	7/10	10/10	+30.0%
Word Problems	7/11	7/11	0%
Money	9/11	9/11	0%
Measurement	15/23	17/23	+8.7%
Time	9/19	10/19	+5.3%

and learning style evaluations—are considered more formal than informal forms of assessment, but they can be administered in the home by the parent, under the supervision of an examiner. Finally, parents can develop and administer informal tests to their children.

There is signficance in administering individual, one-on-one tests to struggling learners. Luftig[7] states that group-administered tests (e.g., *Stanford Achievement Test-8th edition*[8]) typically given to nondisabled students require that the student "possess[es] strong reading or listening skills as well as skill in following directions and working independently," skills we know that children with disabilities generally do not sufficiently possess. Individually-administered, one-on-one tests also allow the examiner more flexibility and control in making sure that the disabled student understands directions and in giving additional cues and prompts to the student as necessary, all of which should result in a more accurate measure of the child's achievement. On group-administered achievement tests, however, the examiner is *not* allowed to deviate from the scripted instructions in the administration manual.

One other major advantage to one-on-one achievement tests is that test items that encourage the student to guess, which are quite prevalent in group-administered achievement tests, are all but eliminated. For example, spelling test items on group-administered achievement tests typically present the child with four renditions of a spelling word, and he is instructed to pick the one which is spelled correctly. Probability tells us that the child has a 25% chance of guessing the item correctly. One-on-one achievement spelling tests, however, require the child to write out from recall the spelling of each word as they are called out to him.

Psychoeducational Tests

Tests administered in a psychoeducational evaluation include, but are not limited to, measures of intelligence, achievement, adaptive behavior, perceptual-motor skills, speech and language skills, emotional/behavioral skills, attentional skills, and giftedness. All of these tests can be administered to the child at one sitting, or they can be divided across several sessions and days. Each of these major types of tests are described below with specific examples:

Intelligence Tests. Intelligence tests determine the extent of a student's God-given abilities to think, reason, remember, process information, acquire knowledge, and the like. The resulting IQ (intelligence quotient) score is a reflection of the student's *potential* to learn. The most popularly used one-on-one intelligence tests are as follows:

- *Wechsler Intelligence Scale for Children-Third Edition*[9]
- *Stanford-Binet Intelligence Scale*[10]
- *Woodcock-Johnson Psycho-Educational Battery-Tests of Cognitive Ability*[11]
- *Kaufman Assessment Battery for Children*[12]
- *Detroit Test of Learning Aptitude-Third Revision*[13]

Achievement Tests (individual). Achievement tests determine the child's current level of performance in the reading/language arts and mathematics areas. Scores are supposed to reflect what the child has *actually* learned in the academic skill areas, not what he is able to learn. We have listed the most commonly used one-on-on achievement tests below:

- *Wechsler Individual Achievement Test*[14]
- *Woodcock-Johnson Psycho-Educational Battery-Tests of Achievement*[15]
- *Kaufman Assessment Battery for Children*[16]
- *Peabody Individual Achievement Test-Revised*[17]
- *Wide Range Achievement Test-Third Revision*[18]

Adaptive Behavior Scales. Adaptive behavior scales determine the extent that a child can function independently on routine, day-to-day life skills (e.g., eating, dressing, social skills, etc.). This type of test is generally given only if the child's intelligence is significantly below average. One example would be the *AAMR Adaptive Behavior Scale-School-Second Revision.*[19]

Perceptual-Motor Tests. These tests determine how well the student can process (input) information visually or auditorially and then respond (output) in some way (usually by drawing, handwriting, etc.). The two most popular perceptual-motor tests are the *Developmental Test of Visual-Motor Integration-Third Revision*[20] and the *Visual Motor Gestalt Test.*[21] Both of these tests present the student with picture cards that display various geometric shapes (e.g., a square, a cross, a circular array of dots, etc.) and the child is asked to reproduce/draw those shapes on a piece of paper.

Speech/Language Screening Tests. These tests determine whether the child is at-risk for a speech and/or language disorder and whether a more comprehensive evaluation from a speech-language pathologist is warranted. An example of a speech articulation screening measure is the *Secord Test of Minimal Articulation Competence.*[22] An example of a language screening measure would be the *Clinical Evaluation of Language Function-Revised.*[23]

Behavior Rating Scales. Behavior rating scales determine whether a student possesses significant problems in self-control, anxiety/depression, social interaction, psychotic behavior, conduct disorders, etc. Generally, these scales are completed by persons (e.g., parents and/or classroom teachers) who are very familiar with the child and can accurately assess his behavior based on prior observations. One behavior rating scale used by some examiners is the *Revised Behavior Problem Checklist.*[24]

Attention Rating Scales. These rating scales determine whether a child has significant problems in attention, impulsivity and/or hyperactivity, which may be the basis for an attention deficit hyperactivity disorder. An example of this type of measure would be the *Attention Deficit Disorder Evaluation Scale.*[25]

Giftedness Rating Scales. Giftedness rating scales function much like the other types of rating scales. Specifically, giftedness rating scales determine whether a student possesses significant giftedness and talent in a particular domain such as leadership, intelligence, specific academic aptitude, the performing and visual arts, etc. The *Gifted Evaluation Scale*[26] is an example of this type of test.

Diagnostic Skill Tests

There are many specific types of diagnostic skill tests on the market today that cover a variety of major academic skill areas. What follows is a listing of some of the more popularly administered, one-on-one diagnostic tests used by examiners today:

School Readiness Skill Tests.

- *BRIGANCE Diagnostic Comprehensive Test of Basic Skills-Readiness Subtest*[27]
- *Denver II Screening*[28]

General Academic Skills Tests.

- *BRIGANCE Diagnostic Comprehensive Inventory of Basic Skills*[29]
- *Wechsler Individual Achievement Test*[30]

Reading Skill Tests.

- *Durrell Analysis of Reading Difficulty*[31]
- *Gray Oral Reading Test-Revised*[32]
- *Stanford Diagnostic Reading Test*[33]
- *Test of Reading Comprehension: Revised Edition*[34]

Spelling/Writing Skill Tests.

- *Test of Written Spelling-2*[35]
- *Spellmaster Assessment and Teaching System*[36]
- *Test of Written Language*[37]
- *Test of Legible Handwriting*[38]

Mathematics Skill Tests.

- *KeyMath Revised: A Diagnostic Inventory of Essential Mathematics*[39]
- *Diagnostic Mathematics Inventory/Mathematics System*[40]
- *Test of Mathematical Ability*[41]

Progress/Achievement Tests

Generally, one-on-one achievement tests need to be administered to children with disabilities and other struggling learners in order to measure their academic growth and performance over a given period of time. Parents will want to have one-on-one achievement tests administered at least once annually. All one-on-one achievement tests must be administered by a professional examiner or other qualified/licensed educator. Two individually administered achievement tests and their corresponding subtests are discussed below:

- *Wechsler Individual Achievement Test.*[42] A comprehensive battery of subtests that measure the child's achievement across the reading, language arts, and mathematics domains. Specific subtests include basic reading, reading comprehension, spelling, written expression, oral expression, mathematics reasoning, and numerical operations (mathematics computation).
- *Woodcock-Johnson Psycho-Educational Battery-Tests of Achievement.*[43] This one-on-one administered achievement test includes both a standard and supplementary battery that cover a broad array of subtests that assess the child's achievement across the reading, language arts, and mathematics as well as other academic areas. Specific subtests include letter-word identification, passage comprehension, word attack, reading vocabulary, proofing (spelling, word usage, and punctuation), dictation (spelling, word usage, and punctua-

tion), writing samples, writing fluency (handwriting), calculation, applied problems (mathematics), quantitative concepts, science, social studies, and humanities.

Screening Instruments

Children who are truly disabled in some way (i.e., learning disabled, emotionally/ behaviorally disordered, etc.) must meet necessary definitional criteria in order to be classified (see Chapter 2). The fact that there are "minimal" criteria for these different forms of disabilities suggests that not all children who have learning, attention, and/or behavior difficulties will in fact be disabled. Unfortunately, parents may invest hundreds of dollars in a comprehensive in-depth psychological/psychoeducational evaluation only to discover that their child's learning, attention, and/or behavior problems were not serious enough to warrant a disability classification.

Parents can avoid costly testing fees by requesting that screening-type instruments be administered to the child prior to in-depth testing. The concept of screening is used often in the medical field. For example, suppose a patient complains of severe pain in his lower right abdomen. A physician may conclude initially that the person's appendix needs to be removed (which is a screening decision). Until the patient undergoes more comprehensive health assessment, however, the suspected need for an appendectomy cannot be conclusively determined. Screening procedures are also used for other health conditions, including pregnancy and serious illnesses like cancer.

Screening can be done in educational circles much the same way that it is done in the medical field. Under the supervision of a professional examiner, parents can complete rating scale instruments of their child's problem behaviors in the comfort of their homes (i.e., the examiner does not have to be present). These screening-type instruments are commercially-produced and will generate a statistical number which compares the frequency of the child's behaviors with a norm sample of children across the country who have been formally classified as disabled. Because these instruments include statistics, the parents must return the completed rating scales to the professional examiner who will score and interpret the results for the parents. If the child's resulting rating score falls below a certain criterion, then the child is considered "at risk" for that disability.

Home-administered rating scales are not robust enough, though, nor do they include collection of enough varied data, for a definitive decision to be made about whether or not the child has a disability. Only through a follow-up, comprehensive psychological/psychoeducational evaluation can the "suspected" disability be confirmed or rejected. So, based on screening results, parents will be able to decide more confidently whether or not to invest additional dollars into follow-up testing. Screening-type rating scales that parents can complete at home are a wise first step for parents who may be considering assessment for their child. More important, screening-type rating scales require only a small investment of money when compared to the more comprehensive, time-consuming evaluations.

Learning Style Evaluations

A number of factors can influence a child's academic success, for example, the child's mood and attitude toward his school work, the parent-child relationship, the quality of the teaching/curricular materials, and so on. We also know that the instructional environment and all the variables that make up the home classroom setting can enhance or adversely affect school success in children. Although learning, attention, and/or behavioral problems may signal a potential disability, these same difficulties could also be an indication of a mismatch between the child's learning style (i.e., his preferences for learning) and the way his classroom environment is arranged.

A child's preferences for learning can be evaluated through commercially-produced learning style instruments. Like screening-type instruments, learning style instruments (sometimes called "inventories") can be administered in the home by the parents under the supervision of a professional examiner. These instruments identify the child's preferences for (i.e., how much or how little) certain environmental variables such as noise, light, need for structure, visual/auditory/ kinesthetic/tactile learning preferences, etc. Once the learning style instrument is completed, the parent returns it the examiner for scoring and analysis. Findings from this type of testing allow the parent to modify the learning environment so that learning conditions will be maximized for the child. For example, if the child prefers some degree of noise in the background while doing school work, the parent could easily adapt the home learning environment by allowing the child to listen to soft music while working.

Informal Assessment

In addition to screening-type tests and learning style inventories that can be administered in the home, parents can also do some diagnostic skill assessment. This type of informal testing is primarily designed to assist the parent in identifying specific reading, writing, spelling, and mathematics skills that the child may not have mastered which are expected of typical students in the child's corresponding age/grade category. These basic skills are the ones that may be holding the child back from learning grade level or even more advanced skills. Ideally, the parent should probably collaborate with a professional examiner who would be able to administer diagnostic tests on a one-on-one basis. But, as we have alluded earlier, the expense factor may prevent some families from being able to secure professional testing.

Nonetheless, if parents are to remediate deficit academic skills in their children, they must know what specific skills the child has not mastered (For a more detailed discussion of remediation, see Chapter 8). In order for parents to do an informal diagnostic assessment in the home, we suggest they follow these steps:

(1) Locate a "scope and sequence" skills list for the child's current grade placement and all prior grade levels in a particular subject area (many teacher manuals provide such lists; the C. Mercer & A. Mercer[44] book also contains skills lists);

(2) Develop at least three test items that reflect each specific skill;

(3) Administer the items for the different skills to the child (gradually over the course of several weeks);

(4) Remediation lessons should be planned for each specific

skill that the child was not able to demonstrate 100% mastery (i.e., 3/3 correct items).

Qualifications of Examiners

Parents would certainly expect their family physician to hold high credentials and have extensive preparation in the medical field, particularly if their child needed surgery for a serious illness. Similarly, parents will want to employ examiners who are properly qualified and prepared in the event that educational testing and evaluation services are needed. According to Salvia and Ysseldyke,[45] leaders in the field of special education assessment, psychoeducational testing in particular should be conducted by licensed/certified professional examiners. Some of the one-on-one achievement and diagnostic tests, however, may be administered by professional educators who hold bachelor's degrees in special education or others who hold master's degrees. As we discussed earlier, parents would be able in most instances to administer screening-type and learning style instruments in the home under the supervision of an outside examiner.

Choosing a professional examiner can be a difficult task. Unfortunately, Christian circles of people in America are not currently blessed with an overabundance of qualified examiners. In fact, in our experiences and conversations with parents across the country, we have discovered that, for the most part, we don't even have an adequate number of qualified examiners. In reality, there are plenty of "qualified" examiners in most parts of this country, if we define "qualified" to mean only having the necessary college degree(s) and accompanying professional license/certificate. A perusal of our telephone directory in the Greenville, SC area yielded a count of over 50 psychologists, psychiatrists, psycho-therapists, psychoanalysts, counselors, and hypnotherapists, all vying for a piece of the client testing pool.

As Bible-believing Christians, however, we believe that term "qualified" must go beyond mere professional credentials. Our broader connotation of the term "qualified" would include one other, equally important criteria, and that is whether or not the examiner is a professing Christian. Some parents may not be too concerned about whether the examiner is a Christian. But the field of special education assessment, like most other aspects of the public educational sector in this country, reeks with secular humanistic philosophy and practices.

For example, many secular psychologists, psychiatrists, and diagnosticians believe in prescribing treatments or therapy such as life space interviewing[46] for students with serious behavioral problems. Treatments like these have as a basic underlying premise that the child is *not* ultimately responsible and accountable for his own behavior. Clearly, treatments that make such assumptions are unscriptural and have no place in the repertoire of potential resources for Christian home educators. We believe that, if these examiners believe in treatments/therapies that run counter to the truths in God's Word, then their identification and testing practices may also reflect actions that are humanistic and outside the boundaries of truth.

We recommend, therefore, that parents employ five specific criteria in selecting an examiner to administer tests to their children who have or are suspected of having a disability. One is to ensure, if at all possible, that the examiner is a Christian. Recently, this writer was conversing via telephone with a home educator from the state of Ohio who was interested in employing the author to evaluate his child whom he thought may possibly have a learning disability. The father asked many questions regarding the specific types of tests that would be administered and how much time it would take and so on. The conversation lasted for almost thirty minutes, and as we were about to conclude, the father gently and politely asked, "Oh, by the way, are you a Bible-believing Christian?", to which the author responded joyfully, "Yes!"

The second criterion is to determine whether or not the examiner is friendly toward and understanding of parents who desire to teach their children at home, particularly those parents who have chosen to be full-time home educators. Our experience has been that many, if not most, secular professional examiners are strong advocates for the public system of education in America. We have personally read test reports from some professional examiners who have chastised parents for wanting to teach their children at home. Clearly, parents will want to employ an examiner who is amiable toward their efforts of home education. Once parents have exhausted their own personal searches in this area and still come up empty-handed, consider making contact with the following organizations/agencies for names of professional examiners who are more friendly toward home teachers:

- Home School Legal Defense Association's Special Education Department (See Appendix A);
- NATHHAN (National Challenged Homeschoolers Associated Network—See Appendix A);
- Individual state home school organizations (A list can be provided by contacting *The Teaching Home*—See Appendix A); and
- Local home education support groups.

The third criterion is to determine whether the examiner has an advanced degree in a field that is directly related to special education assessment (e.g., school psychology, special education, etc.). Although holding the highest advanced degree (i.e., an earned doctorate such as a Ph.D. or Ed.D.) would be best, there are some examiners who hold only master's degrees and are also very qualified to do this type of testing and assessment.

The fourth criterion for choosing an examiner would be to make sure the examiner holds some type of license or certificate from a legitimate national, regional, or state level certifying board/agency. Many, if not most, school psychologists are licensed by the departments of education in their respective state. Others may hold licenses or certificates from a national board (e.g., National Association of Certified School Psychologists). Although not as common as in earlier years, there are a still a few states that offer professional certificates in the field of educational diagnostics. Certified educational diagnosticians more often than not will have backgrounds in the field of special education and extensive classroom teaching experience with disabled students.

Finally, checking to see if the examiner holds memberships in professional organizations (e.g., Council for Exceptional Children, Council for Educational Diagnostic Services, National Council for

Educational Measurement, American Psychological Association) offers some evidence that the examiner is receiving continuing education and preparation in the field of assessment. Most of these professional organizations will publish journals and periodicals that disseminate current research, practices, and policies on how students should be evaluated.

As we mentioned earlier, professional testing can be expensive, particularly psychological/psychoeducational assessment, which can range from a few hundred to a thousand dollars or more. Parents should be aware that their local public schools, under federal mandates stipulated in the 1975 Public Law 94-142, the Educational of All Handicapped Children Act, must provide free testing to any and all referred children, whether or not they are presently enrolled in that public school.

We strongly caution parents to steer clear of this type of free testing, though, for a number of reasons. One, the confidentiality that most parents treasure will be violated, to say the least, since public school officials will have access to the child's scores after the assessment is completed. Two, the school psychologist who tests your child will in all likelihood not be a Christian, which means that, in addition to having conerns about the examiner's integrity, the parent will have to endure secular, humanistic recommendations as far as treatment or service options for the child that will surely run counter to our Christian values and faith.

Three, public school officials will probably feel some sense of "ownership" of the child after the free testing and evaluation, and they may place undue pressure on the family with regard to receiving the public school special education services for the child. Parents who subsequently receive any of the free services from their local public schools may be in danger of "legal entanglement," if litigation ensues down the road (Parents should contact the Home School Legal Defense Association regarding the entanglement issue).

Given these three major limitations, we recommend that parents, particularly those who are full-time home educators, employ private examiners for all their testing needs. To take advantage of free testing services from the public schools may be financially convenient for the immediate, but it may also mean having to "pay the piper" (i.e., the public school system) dearly later on.

How Often Should Students be Tested?

Determining when a student should be tested is based in part on the type of testing desired. For example, if a parent suspects that a child may have a disability, then the earlier a psychological/ psychoeducational evaluation is done, the sooner special education interventions and remediation efforts can be implemented. Once an initial evaluation has been conducted and the child is found to have a disability, then the consensus of professional opinion is that the child should be reevaluated within every three-year period through his high school years. Special education law (P.L. 94-142) refers to this as a triennial review.

Triennial evaluations are necessary, even for home educated students with disabilities, for two reasons. One reason is that we want to determine if there has been any change in the child's abilities and achievement. If so, then it may be necessary to modify or remove the child's particular disability classification altogether. A second reason triennial evaluations are necessary is that the type of special education services and/or treatments may need to be adjusted. It may be that the child initially was classified as having a severe form of a disability, which called for intensive special education programming. Yet upon a triennial evaluation, it could be determined that the student still has a disability, but there has been considerable improvement to the point that a less intensive form of service delivery is needed, for example, special education programming only part of the school day.

A diagnostic skill evaluation should always follow a psychoeducational evaluation. But home educators may desire to have diagnostic skill evaluations done more frequently (e.g., every other year), particularly if the parent is using the specific informa- tion on the child's strengths and weaknesses as a basis for design- ing the child's individual education plan (IEP). If the parents want a more complete documentation and record of the child's annual progress, an annual diagnostic evaluation may be desired. Whether or not the parent chooses an annual diagnostic evaluation, one-on- one achievement tests for progress checks should probably be annually, just as nondisabled students may typically receive annual achievement tests.

We believe that the frequency with which a parent has any type of special education testing conducted should be guided by three principles. The first is to follow carefully all testing requirements that the state may have regarding parents who teach their children at home. States vary on their testing requirements, and there may be more rigorous testing requirements for students who have documented disabilities. Pennsylvania,[47] for example, requires that all children educated at home in grades three, five, and eight take "nationally normed standardized achievement tests in reading/ language arts and mathematics..." Again, we suggest that our readers consult with the Home School Legal Defense Association for information on individual state testing requirements.

A second guiding principle is that the parent should have regular testing and evaluation done with enough frequency to produce sufficient documentation of the child's progress under the home instructional program, should litigation occur in the future. Our experience as special educators has been that proving the effectiveness of teaching disabled students in conventional educational settings hinges primarily on progress that can be documented through regular testing and evaluation, although there is increasing attention being given to the portfolio concept (i.e., gathering samples of the child's school work products) for documentation of child progress. If legal action does ensue, the court could certainly ask for formal test data on the child as evidence of a parent's effort to educate the child properly in the home.

The volatility of the field of special education and ever increasing media attention given to minorities, including persons with disabilities, may suggest to parents that at least regular or perhaps more frequent testing and evaluation for documentation purposes should be the wise order of the day. Somerville,[48] a senior attorney with the Home School Legal Defense Association, offers this advice:

> With so much of the [special education] law unclear, it is critical to focus on the facts in any court case. Home- schooling *works* for children with special needs. If we can put an expert witness on the stand to testify that the family

is doing a good job and getting good results, we can win. If we can't, we are likely to lose, no matter what the law says.

It naturally follows, then, that the expert witness may be able to make a more compelling case that parents are getting good results from home instruction if some formal test data are available on the child's progress.

As we have noted earlier, formal, professional testing can be expensive, and it is not easy to balance your family's resources against the legal risks. We strongly recommend that parents who are full-time home educators consider joining the Home School Legal Defense Association. HSLDA attorneys will be able to provide its member parents with individualized legal advice with regard to seeking professional testing while taking into account the family's financial resources and the peculiarities of the parents' respective state law regarding testing for disabled children.

The last guiding principle is for home special educators to have as much testing and assessment done on their children as is personally preferable for them. Some parents need the encouragement that frequent testing can give, for results from testing can speak to the effectiveness of the home instructional program for struggling learners and whether or not the parents are successfully remediating and ameliorating learning, attention, and/or behavioral problems. Other parents may desire more regular and/or frequent testing so that they can make adjustments in the child's home instructional program more readily. After all, our children will be changing as they grow and develop, and for the better we hope. When testing and evaluation is conducted regularly as it should be, then the parent will be able to make the important and necessary changes in instruction based on changes in learning and behavior that are objectively measured from tests.

---

[1]J. Sutton (1993b)
[2]Vergason (1990), p. 63
[3]Stephens (1977)
[4]Brigance (1983)
[5]Woodcock & Johnson (1989)
[6]Connally (1988)
[7]Luftig (1987), p. 60
[8]Psychological Corporation (1992a)

[9]Psychological Corporation (1991)
[10]Thorndike, Hagen, & Sattler (1995)
[11]Woodcock & Johnson (1989)
[12]A. Kaufman & N. Kaufman (1983)
[13]Hammill (1991)
[14]Psychological Corporation (1992b)
[15]Woodcock & Johnson (1989)
[16]A. Kaufman & N. Kaufman (1983)
[17]Markwardt (1989)
[18]Wilkinson (1993)
[19]Lambert, Nihira, & Leland (1993)
[20]Beery (1989)
[21]Bender (1938)
[22]Secord (1981)
[23]Semel, Wiig, & Secord (1989)
[24]Quay & Peterson (1983)
[25]McCarney (1989)
[26]McCarney (1987)
[27]Brigance (1983)
[28]Frankenburg, Dodds, Archer, Bresnick, Maschaa,
    Edelman, & Shapiro (1990)
[29]Brigance (1983)
[30]Psychological Corporation (1992b)
[31]Durrell & Catterson (1980)
[32]Wiederholt & Bryant (1992)
[33]Karlsen & Gardner (1985)
[34]Brown, Hammill, & Wiederholt (1986)
[35]Larsen & Hammill (1986)
[36]Greenbaum (1987)
[37]Hammill & Larsen (1988)
[38]Larsen & Hammill (1989)
[39]Connally (1988)
[40]Gessell (1983)
[41]Brown & McEntire (1984)
[42]Psychological Corporation (1992b)
[43]Woodcock & Johnson (1989)
[44]C. Mercer & A. Mercer (1994)
[45]Salvia & Ysseldyke (1991)
[46]Heuchert & Long (1980)
[47]Pennsylvania Act 169, cited in H. Richman &
    S. Richman (1993)
[48]Somerville (1994), p. 1

BLUEPRINT FOR INSTRUCTION

M ost of us can testify that, at least once in our lives, we have observed a building that was the result of faulty planning. Perhaps the builder had not anticipated the costs involved and ran out of money. Or perhaps he decided to take the "plan as you go" route, resulting in a mass of piecemeal designs that lacked unity and had structural problems. Whatever the reason, the lack of planning is obvious to all who pass by, and the time and money spent were not well invested. On the other hand, adequately planned buildings are structurally sound, functional in layout, and pleasing to the eye. The time and money invested in the blueprint will pay off when the builder carries out the plan.

The task of educating a learner with limitations is monumental. However, the teacher can greatly simplify the task if she invests time in a carefully constructed plan. Special educators refer to such a plan as the *individualized education plan* (IEP). In essence, the IEP documents the level at which the child is currently functioning and the educational and behavioral goals and objectives for a specific period, usually a school year.

Federal Law requires an IEP for students receiving special education services within the public school system. Legislators intended to ensure that students removed from the regular curriculum would receive meaningful instruction tailored to meet individual needs. So if the IEP is a legal requirement for public school special educators, does the teaching parent of a child with learning limitations need to write an IEP? Although the parent may not be bound legally to have an IEP on the child, there are several good reasons for having one.

The primary purpose for an IEP is planning. The struggling learner will often need significant modifications to the regular curriculum, not to mention remediation in one or more of the basic academic skill areas (e.g., reading, spelling, writing, and/or mathematics). For the most part, these children will need programs of instruction carefully tailored to their unique needs. The parent must plan carefully the kinds of changes in curriculum and teaching methods that will help the child to succeed. Without a carefully formulated plan, the teacher may wander aimlessly from one material or approach to another and be prone to "shoot from the hip." Debbie Mills,[1] home educating mother of a disabled child, says that, "When there are no textbooks to work through, the I.E.P. becomes the curriculum."

Another important reason for writing an IEP involves documentation. If someone should question whether the home educated child were receiving an appropriate education, the IEP documents the plans that will meet the child's specific needs. As the parent carries out the IEP, it then provides documentation of goals and objectives that the student has met. Somerville,[2] of the Home School Legal Defense Association, believes that, "even though IEPs are not necessary for homeschooling families, good documentation is still a must." This documentation may prove to be valuable in case of a legal challenge.

Elements of IEP

So, what does writing an IEP involve? Based on instructions contained in Public Laws 94-142 (The Education of All Handicapped Children Act, 1975) and 101-476 (The Individuals with Disabilities Education Act, 1990), the required elements of a properly-written IEP for public educators include the following information about the child:

- present level of educational performance
- annual goals
- short-term instructional objectives
- evaluation criteria/plans

- type/amount of special education and/or related services
- extent of inclusion with nondisabled students
- transition plans/services for adolescents
- beginning and ending dates of program

Although these elements are required by law for public educators who are developing and writing IEPs for students with disabilities, they are *not* required of those who are educating children outside the realm of public, federally-funded schools, which would include home schools. If your home education program ever comes under legal challenge, however, your IEP may be more credible and carry more weight if it follows the pattern established by federal law. Therefore, we recommend that parents seriously consider following these elements in preparing home IEPs.

A careful look at each of these IEP elements allows one to conclude that they are reasonable and essential if the IEP is to describe the tailor-made program of the struggling learner in a comprehensive way. We believe that parents are capable of developing their own IEPs, although some may choose to get some assistance from a special education consultant. In the paragraphs below, we provide an explanation of each of these IEP elements.

Present Level of Educational Performance

The present level of educational performance, written in paragraph form, describes the strengths and weaknesses of the child academically. It may also include social and emotional/behavioral characteristics. In addition to describing in a general way the child's cognitive abilities (i.e., his learning potential), this section of the IEP will probably include statements describing his math and reading levels, abilities in oral and written expression, and progress in the content areas. The summary may include the child's learning and modality preferences (i.e., visual, auditory, kinesthetic, and/or tactile). A variety of sources provide this information including psychological/psychoeducational evaluations, diagnostic evaluations, recent achievement tests, and parent/teacher observations.

Annual Goals

The summary of the present level of performance is a springboard into the annual goals and short term objectives. The child's present abilities help determine his goals in each area of need that he may have for the coming year. For example, it would not be unusual for a child's IEP to contain annual goal statements in the major academic areas such as reading, spelling, and mathematics. But a child's IEP could also contain an annual goal statement in other areas such as adaptive behavior (if the child is developmentally disabled). Parents who are Christians may even want to include an annual goal statement for Bible instruction. Whatever the case, the number of annual goal statements will vary from one child to the next, depending on the specific areas of need that each child may have. A child may have significant spiritual needs that need to be addressed and for which an annual goal will need to be stated on the IEP. We refer our readers to an IEP approach that emphasizes the teaching of Biblical/spiritual concepts in a book on Christian special education entitled, *Special Education: A Biblical Approach*.[3]

Each goal statement should describe what the child should probably be able to do by the end of the year. In short, the annual goal is simply an instructional target. It is a statement of where the teaching parent expects the child to be, educationally speaking, at the end of the program period. A typical mathematics goal statement for a student with a mild disability and currently achieving at a grade equivalent of 4.0 in mathematics might be "Tommy will earn a grade score of 5.0 in numerical operations on the *Wechsler Individual Achievement Test* by June, 1995."

Short-term Instructional Objectives

Short-term objectives are the steps that lead to the accomplishment of an annual goal. These steps or short-term objectives might be what the child could accomplish in a few weeks or a month. In other words, the teaching parent may need to spend several weeks addressing one instructional objective with a child by presenting and teaching the skill from different instructional angles. By completing all the short-term objectives in a given area, the student will have met his annual goal. Parents will need to formulate anywhere from five to ten instructional objectives per goal statement. An example of a typical short-term objective that leads to Tommy's mathematics goal might be, "Given a set of ten problems presented via computer, Tommy will be able to add two-digit numbers with regrouping at 90% accuracy.

The goals and objectives contained on a student's IEP need only address the areas in which the student has learning deficits. For example, if the student is functioning on the expected level in spelling, then IEP goals and objectives in spelling are not necessary since the student will be following the scope and sequence of skills in a regular curriculum. In order to identify the specific areas in which a child has deficits, the parent will have to draw from the student's *diagnostic* test results. This means that the parent will either have to administer her own informal diagnostic tests on the child or have a professional administer one-on-one diagnostic tests (see Chapter 5).

Plans and Criteria for Evaluation

Next the IEP must show plans for evaluation of these objectives. The plan should show *how* the parent plans to evaluate the student's performance (e.g., parent-made test, commercially produced test, timed test, flashcards, oral questioning, parent observation, etc.) for stated objectives and *what level* of mastery the student must attain (e.g., 90% accuracy, 50 correct responses in 3 minutes, etc.). The level of mastery may be established in advance by the Department of Education in the state that the parent resides. Members of the Home School Legal Defense Assocation should consult their state's attorney regarding this matter.

Special Education/Related Services

A statement of specific educational services lists *what* areas need remediation (or special education), the types of related services (such as speech or physical therapy), *who* will provide each of the services, *where* the service will take place, and *when* and *how long* the service will be delivered.

Extent of Inclusion with Nondisabled

Students with disabilities need opportunities where they can mingle, play, and interact with other nondisabled children so that they can transfer what they are learning in the home, particularly social aspects of learning (e.g., getting along with others). The IEP should include the times when the child will be involved with other children outside the one-on-one, highly individualized home teaching environment. For example, a parent may teach a daily group lesson to all of her children in such areas as Bible or social studies. The child may attend a weekly group science, music, and/ or art lesson at a neighbor's house, a weekly group physical education activity at the YMCA, or take monthly field trips with other children. These should be listed as specifically as possible on the IEP.

Transition Services

Students moving upon graduation from formal education into the world of work or to college (typically referred to as "transition") is difficult enough for those students who do not struggle, but for children with disabilities it can be an extremely traumatic time. This transition element was only recently required by Public Law 101-476 and has been added to the original list of seven IEP elements that were specified in Public Law 94-142. Thus, the intent of the transition services provision is to stipulate the plans on how the student will be transitioned. For example, parents may state in the IEP that part of the student's educational program during his junior and senior year of high school would be securing a job training/internship position with an employer in the community, where the student would be able to learn specific job skills. Salvia and Ysseldyke[4] indicate that the Individuals with Disabilities Education Act, a federal special education law, requires transitional services for students when they reach the age of 16.

Beginning and Ending Dates

Finally, the IEP must also include the dates that services are expected to begin and the proposed date of completion. Most IEP's also include projected dates for beginning each of the objectives and some space to document completion of an objective. Additionally, some individuals wish to specify what special methods or materials they plan to use to accomplish each objective. For example, for a child with the objective to learn his 0-3 multiplication facts to a level of 50 in 3 minutes, the parent may specify that the child will use Fernald/VAKT method (see Chapter 8), flashcards, and a particular mathematics computer program. The extent of detail in this area may vary from one home teacher to another. Are the goals and objectives written in stone? Even the most carefully made plans may need some adjustment. The parent may find his expectations were too high (the student did not reach the goal this year) or too low (the student reached it before the year was over). The intent of the federal law with regard to IEPs is to leave some degree of flexibility in adjusting the student's IEP goals and objectives. He is not held accountable if the goals are not met so long as a good faith effort is made in trying to achieve them. If the parent discovers early on that a particular goal was quite unrealistic, he may amend it during the school year. Again, parents should probably check with their respective states (or the HSLDA) to determine for sure how much flexibility they have in making adjustments.

Formats for IEP's vary widely from one locality to another; however, they all should contain the same required basic elements. Developing the IEP will involve time and careful consideration, and, as we indicated earlier, may require some degree of professional assessment, if the parent does not intend to conduct informal diagnostic assessment in the home. However, the time and effort invested should result in providing a blueprint of instruction that is geared to the child's unique needs and one which should foster more observable progress for that child in the end.

We have chosen for illustration purposes an IEP that one home educating father and mother used for their son who has spina bifida (assistance in developing this IEP was provided by a special education consultant).

---

[1]Mills (1995), p. 20
[2]Somerville (1994), p. 1
[3]J. Sutton (1993c)
[4]Salvia & Ysseldyke (1991)

Individualized Educational Plan

Student: Brian Scott Davis
Age: 12 yrs. 3 mos.
School: Davis Home School
Parents: David & Jennifer Davis
Address: RD 3 Box 577-B, Anytown, USA
Related Services: Physical therapy;
                                Occupational therapy

Disability: PD
Grade: 5.0
School Year: 1994-95
Consultant: John P. Doe
Phone: 999-999-9999
Date Written: 9-28-94

PRESENT LEVEL OF PERFORMANCE:

Brian's most recent psycho-educational evaluation done in 1990 measured his intelligence quotient (IQ) to be 69 (K-ABC Test). However, in 1989, Brian's verbal IQ was measured to be 88 on the WISC-R. From the diagnostic educational evaluation conducted by this consultant on 6-13-94, Brian's current grade scores on the WIAT achievement test across the academic subject areas were as follows:

Basic Reading	5.1	Mathematics Reasoning	K.8
Spelling	2.8	Reading Comprehension	2.9
Numerical Operations	1.4	Listening Comprehension	1.3
Oral Expression	2.4	Written Expression	2.1

STRENGTHS/WEAKNESSES:

Although God has been pleased to allow Brian to have spina bifida, which certainly disables him both physically and academically, Brian possess a number of strengths that will surely allow him to compensate for those weaknesses. For example, Brian has excellent social skills. He is able to establish and maintain excellent positive relationships with people, both young and old, easily. Brian also has unusually good communication skills. His ability to verbalize well should serve him well as he progresses through school in the years to come, as he does have difficulties in his written communication skills.

BEHAVIORAL OBSERVATIONS:

Brian exhibits very good self-control of behavior. He responds well to authority. He presents himself to be a young boy of unusual maturity. He knows when to ask for help and is not embarrassed doing this. This suggests to those who are looking on that he has accepted his disability as from the Lord.

INITIATION/TERMINATION OF SPECIAL EDUCATION SERVICES:

Brian's special education services will be delivered one-on-one by his parents and will begin the present year at the signing of this document and terminates June 30, 1995.

EXTENT OF SPECIAL EDUCATION SERVICES:

Subject	Time/Daily	Location	Teacher
Reading	20 min.	Home	Mrs. Davis
Spelling	20 min.	Home	Mrs. Davis
Written expression	30 min.	Home	Mrs. Davis
Mathematics	30 min.	Home	Mrs. Davis

EXTENT OF MAINSTREAMING EFFORTS:

Since Brian's home school special education program represents a unique educational setting that is highly individualized (i.e., parent and student), mainstreaming efforts will obviously be limited compared to students educated in conventional school settings. Nonetheless, Mrs. Davis recognizes the necessity of giving Brian opportunities to be integrated with other nondisabled individuals in order for him to be able to transfer what he is learning to broader contexts. Thus, the following activities have been planned to address this need:

Activity	Time/Week	Supervisor
Piano lessons	30 minutes	Miss Jennifer Cook
Sunday School/Church	3-4 hours	Mr. John Smith
Children's Choir	90 minutes	Mrs. Debbie Jones
Community soccer games	1 hour	Mr. and Mrs. Davis
Community basketball games	1 hour	Mr. and Mrs. Davis
Chapel with Christian school	45 minutes	Mrs. Davis

TRANSITION SERVICES:

Disabled students who are in their high school years and approaching graduation from high school need transition services. The purpose of a transition plan is to allow for smooth entry of the young adult into the community/job world, if the student is not anticipating post-secondary education. Yet for those disabled young people who are planning on furthering their education (e.g., community/ technical college or baccalaureate, four-year college degree program), a plan still needs to be developed to help them bridge their exit from high school to the college setting. No transition plan is needed for Brian at this time.

Reading

ANNUAL GOAL: Brian will improve his overall reading achievement to a grade score of 6.0 on the WIAT achievement test by June, 1995.

INSTRUCTIONAL OBJECTIVES:	TYPE EVALUATION:	DATE COMPLETED:
1. Brian will be able to read age-appropriate words with short vowel sounds "i" and "o" with 100% accuracy.	_____	_____
2. Brian will be able to read age-appropriate words with long vowel sounds "e", "i", and "u" with 100% accuracy.	_____	_____
3. Brian will be able to read and pronounce age-appropriate words with proper syllabication and accent with 100% accuracy.	_____	_____
4. Brian will be able to answer questions from reading passage that have to do with recognizing stated cause and effect with at least 90% accuracy.	_____	_____
5. Brian will be able to answer questions from reading passages that have to do with comparing and contrasting with at least 90%accuracy.	_____	_____
6. Brian will be able to answer questions from reading passages that have to do with predicting events and outcomes with at least 90% accuracy.	_____	_____
7. Brian will be able to answer questions from reading passages that have to do with recognizing stated detail with at least 90% accuracy.	_____	_____

Evaluation Codes: OQ=oral questions; TMT=teacher-made test; CMT=commercially-made test; TO=teacher observation.

Spelling

ANNUAL GOAL: Brian will improve his spelling achievement to a grade score of 5.0 on the WIAT achievement test by June, 1995.

INSTRUCTIONAL OBJECTIVES:	TYPE EVALUATION:	DATE COMPLETED:
1. Brian will be able to spell words with the following suffixes with at least 90% accuracy: -n,-less,-vies,-or,-ous,-ance,-ant,-ence,-ible,-ian,-ation,-ity,-ize	_____	_____
2. Brian will be able to spell words with the following prefixes with at least 90% accuracy: de-,en-,ir-,anti-,semi-	_____	_____
3. Brian will be able to spell all of the days of the week with at least 100% accuracy.	_____	_____
4. Brian will be able to spell all of the months of the year with at least 100% accuracy.	_____	_____
5. Brian will be able to spell homophone words (e.g., write/right; eight/ate, etc.) with at least 90% accuracy.	_____	_____

Evaluation Codes: OQ=oral questions; TMT=teacher-made test; CMT=commercially-made test; TO=teacher observation.

Written Expression

ANNUAL GOAL: Brian will improve his written expression achievement to a
grade score of 5.0 on the WIAT achievement test by June, 1995.

INSTRUCTIONAL OBJECTIVES:	TYPE EVALUATION:	DATE COMPLETED:
1. Brian will be able to take a topic of interest and generate three main points with several subpoints with at least 100% accuracy.	____	____
2. Brian will be able to write complete sentences including subject, verb, and direct object with 100% accuracy.	____	____
3. Brian will be able to capitalize words in sentences that represent groups of people (e.g., Campfire Girls, Boy Scouts, etc.) with 100% accuracy.	____	____
4. Brian will be able to capitalize words in sentences that represent government groups, business firms, and product brand names with 100% accuracy.	____	____
5. Brian will be able to place a comma between city and state in sentences with 100% accuracy.	____	____
6. Brian will be able to place periods after initials in names in sentences with 100% accuracy.	____	____
7. Brian will be able to place apostrophes for possessive nouns in sentences with 100% accuracy.	____	____

Evaluation Codes: OQ=oral questions; TMT=teacher-made test;
CMT=commercially-made test; TO=teacher observation.

Mathematics

ANNUAL GOAL: Brian will improve his overall mathematics achievement to a grade score of 5.0 on the WIAT achievement test by June, 1995.

INSTRUCTIONAL OBJECTIVES:	TYPE EVALUATION:	DATE COMPLETED:
1. Brian will be able to estimate a given line segment alongside a rule in inches with at least 90% accuracy.	_____	_____
2. Brian will be able to solve a word problem requiring knowledge of the value of coins(penny, dime) with at least 90% accuracy.	_____	_____
3. Brian will be able to solve a one-step addition problem (when read to him) with at least 90% accuracy.	_____	_____
4. Brian will be able to solve a one-step subtraction problem involving money with at least 90% accuracy.	_____	_____
5. Brian will commit his addition and subtraction facts to memory and be able to reproduce them in spoken or written form with 100% accuracy.	_____	_____
6. Brian will be able to add a row of three one-digit numbers presented horizontally with 100% accuracy.	_____	_____
7. Brian will be able to subtract two two-digit numbers that require no renaming with 100% accuracy.	_____	_____

Evaluation Codes: OQ=oral questions; TMT=teacher-made test; CMT=commercially-made test; TO=teacher observation.

ACCEPTANCE OF/AGREEMENT TO IMPLEMENT IEP

I accept this IEP as the educational plan that will best meet the needs of my child. Furthermore, as my child's home teacher, I agree to abide by the requirements and stipulations of this IEP during the course of the present school year and will implement it by planning individualized instruction for my child that will be based on the stated instructional objectives herein.

_____

David or Jennifer Davis
Home School Parent/Teacher

_____

John P. Doe
Special Education Consultant*

_____

Date

*Note: No consultant signature is necessary. Parents' signature designates a self-contract.

Chapter

7

CONSULTANT SERVICES

S eeking the advice and counsel of others who may be wiser and more experienced (Proverbs 12:15) is an important character trait. It is crucial for parents who teach struggling learners to possess this character trait, because a parent's willingness to share and receive teaching ideas and suggestions may be exactly what is needed for a child to be more successful. We have found that parents who are full-time home educators have recognized the value of seeking advice and counsel from others. This is evident in their participation in hundreds of local home school support groups across the country and the well-attended annual home school conventions and curriculum fairs that now exist in virtually every state.

Not all parents may have access to a local support group, though, and not all conventions and curriculum fairs provide speakers who address the needs and concerns that parents of struggling learners may have. Parents, therefore, will need to search out other resources for help from time to time. One way to get the extra help and assistance needed to teaching struggling learners at home is by collaborating with an educational consultant.[1] Janet (Wayne) Walker,[2] special needs coordinator with the Home School Legal Defense Association, reports that, "there is a growing network of professionals,... who are willing and interested in assisting families in the areas of testing, educational counseling, and the various therapies."

Justification for Consultants

By definition[3], a consultant is one who "gives professional or technical advice." Clearly, based on what we have presented to this point, teaching struggling learners requires a parent to have skills that go beyond what would be expected in teaching typical learners. The field of special education can be a highly technical one, and parents who choose to educate a struggling learner at home, particularly if the child has a disability, may need professional advice and assistance on occasion and perhaps on a regular basis at first. If parents carefully choose professional special educators as their consultants, then they should expect to receive the technical and instructional assistance they will need to provide an appropriate instruction in the home that will meet the child's unique needs.

Although the technical assistance aspect in and of itself is sufficient justification for having a special education consultant, there is one additional, perhaps more compelling reason for parents to have and retain a special education consultant—legal support. HSLDA[4] provides the following admonition:

> Because of the legal complexities involved in dealing with schools and government agencies, one of the **safest** things you can do to protect your home school is to obtain the services of a special needs educational consultant. This consultant would be someone who could, in the event HSLDA was called upon to defend your home school, serve as an objective expert witness...

If parents are collaborating with a consultant on a regular basis, the consultant should be able provide the necessary documentation and testimony to corroborate the parents' home teaching efforts, if litigation ensues. Grace Flynn,[5] a home educating mother of a son who has Down Syndrome, believes that obtaining assistance from an special education consultant, "is for our benefit, so that we do a good job and are not found wanting in the event of a court case."

Candidates for Consultants

HSLDA[6] believes that a qualified special education consultant "can be anyone who has either credentials or experience in the same area as [the] child's special need." We believe that the best candidates for special education consultants are those who hold professional credentials (i.e., a college degree and/or licenses or certificates) *and* experience in the field of special education. For the most part, parents should be able to find a well-prepared and well-credentialled special education consultant from one of the following groups: (a) special education teachers currently teaching in public or private/Christian schools; (b) retired special education teachers; (c) learning specialists who operate private clinics; and (d) professors of special education at the university level.

Home educators can secure a special education consultant in a number of ways. Contacting the supervisor of special education at one's public school district and asking if any special education teachers might be interested in serving as consultants would be one option, but we strongly discourage it. A parent's inquiry may signal the public school system that the parent doesn't know what he/she is doing, or possibly that the parent is neglecting the child in an educational sense. In either case, the school system may decide to investigate legally. We recommend that parents first check with local home school support groups or state home school associations who may keep a list of available special education consultants. A second source would be the Home School Legal Defense Association, which maintains a current list of special education consultants from various regions of the country. Thirdly, the National Challenged Homeschoolers Associated Network or NATHHAN (see Appendix A) in Washington state may be able to assist parents in securing special education consultants. Finally, if all else fails, parents might consider making contact with one or more of the private schools in their community to see if they have special education teachers who would be willing to be employed in the after-school hours as consultants.

Services from the Consultant

The effective special education consultant often is able to provide a number of important services, from teaching assistance to evaluation of the child's abilities and progress. Although some consultants may provide more specific services than others, parents will want to make sure that they can secure assistance and/or counsel in any of the following areas as they need them (Note: Parents may need to work with several consultants in order to get all of these services.):

- Testing and evaluation services;
- Individualized educational plan (IEP) development ;
- Curriculum recommendations;
- Instructional modifications;
- Specialized teaching techniques;
- Various educational procedures; and
- Managing behavior/discipline techniques.

An effective special education consultant should be able to provide information and assistance on testing and evaluation services. It is imperative that struggling learners and students with disabilities receive one-on-one testing for a number of important reasons (please refer back to Chapter 5). If the consultant is not certified/licensed to administer these one-on-one tests, then he/she should be able to refer you to a professional examiner who is qualified to do so.

Parents may also wish to see the assistance of the consultant in developing an individualized educational plan (IEP) for the child. The purpose of the IEP is to provide a blueprint of individualized instruction that the child will receive for the school year. Although it is understandable that not all special education consultants will have the necessary credentials to provide testing and evaluation services, we believe that the ability to assist a parent in writing an IEP, based on results from diagnostic testing on the child, is an essential requirement that all special education consultants should have. All home school lessons from a remedial perspective designed by the parent for the child should stem from the instructional objectives written on the child's IEP (See Chapter 6).

In addition to testing services and IEP development, the special education consultant will also advise the parent on instructional matters such as choosing the most appropriate curricular materials for the child. The most important principle to keep in mind here is to make sure that the child is placed on curricular materials that are at his/her current achievement functioning level. For example, although a child with a learning disability may have completed three years of school beyond a kindergarten year (i.e., he is in third grade), his current achievement/functioning level may only be comparable to average students at the first grade level. In conjunction, the special education consultant should be able to advise the parent on what instructional modifications and accommodations should be provided in order that the child can most effectively learn in the home school and which teaching techniques would be more appropriate (See Chapters 9 and 10).

Another service provided by the consultant should be advice on how to evaluate the child's daily progress and how to schedule instructional time. Struggling learners and children with disabilities will need more frequent daily evaluations on their mastery of material. In addition, with the child's unique needs in mind, the consultant should recommend the amount of time necessary for remediation each day and how much time should be allocated for teaching the commercially-produced, adopted curriculum (See Chapter 11).

One final service of the consultant is advising the home teacher on ways to manage the child's behavior more effectively. Managing behavior effectively in children with disabilities is a critical prerequisite to their eventual progress and mastery of academic skills. The consultant should be a master behavior manager and should be able to coach the parent in designing techniques and strategies that will resolve behavior problems in the home school (See Chapter 12).

Contacts With Your Consultant

A parent's very first contact with the consultant should probably be used to get clarification/documentation of the consultant's credentials, expectations, specific services, and fees. Parents who are full-time home educators will need to make sure that they discuss early on with the consultant any specific requirements for teaching children with disabilities in the home that are mandated by the state. Some states are more demanding and rigorous in their requirements than others. Don't expect the consultant to have this information readily, though, especially if the consultant is from out-of-state. Ultimately, the parents are responsible to obtain their own state's requirements and to make sure that services provided by the consultant will meet those requirements.

Scott Somerville,[7] an attorney with HSLDA, recommends that a parent's additional contacts with the consultant should be done periodically throughout the school year. In general, when it comes to instructional matters, the more a parent makes contact with his/her special education consultant, the more efficient the home education program will probably be. Consultants vary on the minimum number of times they expect parents to make contact with them. Specifically, HSLDA recommends that the consultant make contact with the family a minimum of four times during the school year.[8]

The number of contacts will also vary according to the experience of the parent and the severity of the child's disability. For parents who are novices at teaching children with disabilities in the home and/or whose child may have a severe/profound disability (e.g., severe mental retardation), we recommend that there be monthly contact with the consultant during the course of the first home school year. For the second school year, we recommend that the parents make contact with their consultant every other school month (e.g., September, November, January, etc.). For the third and succeeding school years, four contacts with the consultant should be sufficient, provided the child's progress is at a level that is satisfactory to the parent. In the long run, each parent will have to decide how many contacts he/she will personally need to feel comfortable in providing appropriate instruction to the struggling learner or disabled child.

Forms of Consultation

There are three primary forms of consultation: (a) personal visits; (b) mail/fax; and (c) telephone. Although the best mode of consultation by far is the personal visit, some parents do not have this luxury, for their consultants may not live in the near vicinity. Several hours of driving may separate some parents and their consultants. Thus, two other frequently used modes of consultation are mail/fax and telephone.

Between the telephone and mail/fax forms of consultation, the telephone and fax will be the most expensive, particularly if the phone call is a long distance one. We recommend that for each month of contact between the parent and his/her consultant, that the parent consider sending written information via letter/fax on activities/progress that have occurred in the home program followed by a phone call initiated by the parent to the consultant. The letter/fax should include the following information: (a) daily record of student's performance/grades in the various subject areas—usually reported as a percentage success (see Chapter 11); (b) parent's impressions of progress or lack thereof (probably from a daily journal); and (c) a list of questions regarding instruction that have occurred to the parent throughout the school month. The phone call that follows the letter/fax should be a discussion of recommendations and solutions to the questions of concern that were mailed to the consultant in advance.

Consultation Costs

Special education consultants generally charge a professional fee for their services that is commensurate with their level of professional preparation (i.e., a bachelor's, master's, or doctor's degree in special education). As with fees for testing services, consulting fees can also vary from one part of the country to another, with the higher fees occurring near urban areas. Some consultants may charge fees based on time (i.e., per hour basis), yet others might charge according to the specific job requested (e.g., assisting the parent in developing and writing an IEP). Our experience has been that consultants who hold at least a master's degree will charge a minimum of about $20 per hour of service. Those with doctor's degrees, though, could charge as high as $45 to $75 per hour.

Consultant services will involve an expense for sure. But we believe that, when parents get to the point that they need outside help, the invested money will be worth it all in the long-run. Parrish,[9] a home educating mother of a health impaired son, testifies that, "Consulting special education teachers...[have] helped [me], and the importance of this guidance cannot be stressed enough..."

[1]Lapish (1994)
[2]Walker (1994), p. 40
[3]*American Heritage Dictionary* (1985)
[4]HSLDA (no date), p. 2
[5]Flynn (1994), p. 43
[6]HSLDA (no date), p. 2
[7]Somerville (1994)
[8]HSLDA (no date)
[9]Parrish (1995), p. 44

Chapter

8

MODIFYING INSTRUCTION

S ome parents use commercially-produced educational materials (e.g., textbooks, workbooks, and/or teacher manuals) as the primary vehicle of instruction in their homes. Using a single pre-packaged curriculum or a combination of different curricula may be enough for some students, but it is generally insufficient for struggling learners. Although there are some very good curricula on the market today, curricular materials alone will not be able to meet all the unique needs that a struggling learner may have. More important, home educators should recognize that most curricula are designed for average, typical learners, not learners who may have learning, attention, and/or behavior difficulties. In short, standard commercially-produced, grade-level curricula are simply not enough for struggling learners.[1]

Learners who struggle, particularly those with disabilities, will possess learning deficits in one or more of the major academic areas (i.e., reading, writing, spelling, and mathematics). Thus, instruction that focuses on remediation should be an important part of their daily instruction. But many of these children nonetheless will have an intelligence that falls within the average range, which suggests that they also have the ability to learn from regular curricular materials, as long as these materials are on their functioning level. We believe, then, that the key to effective home education for struggling learners is to tailor-make a program that includes a balance of both *remedial* and *regular* instruction.

Parents will need to provide daily periods of remediation in order to close the learning gaps and give children opportunities to master basic skills that they heretofore have not mastered and which are probably preventing them from learning more complex material. Knowing which skills need to be remediated will require diagnostic testing to be done on the child, either by a professional examiner or through informal assessment by the parent (see Chapter 5). Remedial instruction alone, though, is not enough either. It is also important that we keep these children on a regular course of instruction that is on their *functioning* level, particularly in the subject areas not in need of remediation, so that they can progress along in a normal sequence of instruction that is expected of typical learners.

Determining how much daily instructional time should be spent on remediation versus regular instruction depends largely on the severity of the child's learning problems. For children with mild to moderate learning difficulties, dividing daily instructional time equally between remediation and regular instruction may be best. Yet for those students who have severe learning problems, appropriating a greater amount of daily instruction to remediation may increase the likelihood that learning gaps will be closed sooner.

Regardless of how much emphasis parents place on remedial and/or regular instruction, we know that most struggling learners will have to be taught differently sometimes. Traditional approaches to teaching these children will probably not be effective. Simply presenting information visually or orally through textbooks and workbooks, making assignments, and giving extra time and practice for understanding may be sufficient for average learners, but not for struggling learners. They will need modifications in instruction and specialized teaching methods and approaches in order to succeed at a rate that corresponds with their God-given ability.

The remainder of this chapter will focus on how parents can modify instruction as they teach in the home. We begin with a discussion of how parents can alter their own teaching behavior, which certainly is a major part of the instructional process. We conclude with ideas on how parents can provide modifications and accommodations in instructional materials and the learning environment for learners who struggle.

Teacher Behavior

We believe that home teachers should first evaluate their own teaching behavior before investing the time and effort it will take to implement instructional modifications or specialized teaching methods. It may well be that parents find upon self-evaluation that they will need to alter their teaching behavior in some way. Altering one's "teaching behavior" may seem a bit peculiar to some parents. After all, behavior change is almost always discussed with the student in mind, not the teacher. But researchers have identified a number of teaching behaviors that, when implemented deliberately and systematically by the teacher, will make a significant difference in how children learn.

For example, Nowacek, McKinney, and Hallahan[2] compared teaching behaviors of regular classroom teachers and special education teachers. These researchers discovered that special educators showed *more* of the following teaching behaviors when teaching students with disabilities than did regular teachers in traditional classrooms with nondisabled learners (asterisk "*" indicates significantly more):

- **Monitoring***-the teacher provides careful oversight and supervision of learning experiences for the child, while giving regular assistance and structuring of the child's responses to questions.
- **Questioning**-the teacher asks questions about what was taught in the lesson and questions about the student's work.
- **Praise***-the teacher delivers positive, verbal statements that are reinforcing to the child for acceptable performance and will give a reason for the praise, rather than general, global praise.
- **Positive Regard***-the teacher motivates the child by urging him to work harder, providing him with reassurance that he is moving in the right direction, and recognizes his unique needs that may require various instructional modifications.

Nowacek and her colleagues also discovered that special education teachers showed *approximately the same* amounts of the following teaching behaviors as did regular classroom teachers:

- **States Expectations**-the teacher provides an introduction to the lesson by reviewing with the student, states exactly what will be studied during the lesson, and states precisely what the student will be required to do after the lesson concludes.
- **Makes Assignments**-the teacher brings the lesson to an end by reviewing and summarizing what was taught, checks to make sure that the student understands what was taught, brings likely mistakes to the child's attention, and clearly states instructions for assignment and what she expects of the student.

Finally, Nowacek and her associates found the special education teachers showed *less* of the following teaching behaviors compared to regular classroom teachers (asterisk "*" indicates significantly less):

- **Negative Regard***-the teacher ignores needs of students and shows little tolerance for their characteristic behaviors.
- **Effective Transitions**-the teacher prepares the student for times during the instructional period when different activities will be occurring.

In another teacher effectiveness study, Sutton, McKinney, and Hallahan[3] investigated some of the same teaching behaviors as the prior researchers, but with special education teachers who taught *mildly* disabled students versus special education teachers who taught *severely* disabled students. Highlights of their findings were as follows (asterisk "*" indicates significantly more/less):

- Teachers of severely disabled students **showed more negative regard*** than did teachers of mildly disabled students.
- Teachers of severely disabled students **acknowledged misbehavior more*** than did teachers of mildly disabled students.
- Teachers of severely disabled students **desisted, rebuked, warned, threatened, and punished more*** inattentive and disruptive behavior in severely disabled students than did teachers of mildly disabled students.

- Teachers of severely disabled students **ignored more** inattentive and disruptive behavior than did teachers of mildly disabled students.
- Teachers of mildly disabled students **stated expectations more** than did teachers of severely disabled students.
- Teachers of mildly disabled students **gave more positive regard** than did teachers of severely disabled students.
- Teachers of mildly disabled students **made assignments more** than did teachers of severely disabled students.
- Teachers of mildly disabled students **gave answers more** to student-initiated questions/comments than did teachers of severely disabled students.

Only a handful of other studies to date[4,5,6,7,8,9,10] have examined effective teaching behaviors of teachers who teach students with mild disabilities such as mild mental retardation, learning disabilities, and emotional/behavior disorders. A consensus of statistical findings from these studies reveals that teachers of struggling learners will do significantly more of each of the following for their students:

- **Ask more questions** during a lesson;
- **Allow more trials** in responding correctly to questions;
- **Elicit more correct responses** from students;
- **Tell fewer answers to questions** (which allows students to figure it out on their own);
- **Provide more positive and negative feedback**;
- **Provide more support and encouragement**;
- **Provide shorter lessons**;
- **Provide more concept examples** (for illustration);
- **Provide greater lesson structure** (e.g., objectives, introductions, explanations, summaries, and reviews); and
- **Provide more monitoring of assignments**.

We believe that home teachers who implement these teaching behaviors in their daily instruction will maximize learning success in their children. Concentrating on one or two teaching behaviors per week, rather than trying to implement all of these at once, may be the most effective way of incorporating these into your daily instruction.

Making Modifications and Accommodations

Fouse and Brians[11] contend that, "For many ADD students, all that is needed to help succeed in school are some modifications in assignments and tests." We agree with Fouse and Brians and suggest that modifying and accommodating for instruction is critical to the success of *all* struggling learners, not just ADD students, although some struggling learners may eventually need the additional benefit of instruction presented through different teaching techniques (discussed in Chapters 9 and 10). Generally, modifications are given to a student in order to help him compensate for or work around a barrier or limitation in his life that may be preventing him from learning at optimal levels. We provide a number of examples and ways that parents can provide modifications in the paragraphs that follow.

Regardless of the type or degree of modification the home teacher provides the child, one principle should be kept in mind. Instructional modifications and accommodations are legitimate and appropriate only if academic integrity is preserved and not compromised in the learning process. That is, when modifications give the student an "edge" or advantage rather than allowing him to compensate for and work around the barrier of his limitation, then the modification ceases from being of any real educational value to the child. For example, it would be difficult, if not impossible, to justify allowing an ADD student to use a calculator to complete a mathematics assignment, when he has no prior history of learning difficulties in mathematics. Giving him a calculator would in effect reduce the quality of his learning by preventing him from exercising his computational skills.

General Suggestions

One of the most comprehensive collections of instructional modifications that we have identified to date is Cohen's[12] *Instructional Modification Menu* (pp. 103-104). Home teachers will find the ideas contained therein immensely practical and helpful. In addition, a number of instructional modifications and accommodations have been discussed by researchers in several recent studies.[13,14] Many of these ideas are directly applicable to parents who have children with learning difficulties. Consider these accommo-

Instructional Modification Menu

1. Use a study carrel
2. Set-up room dividers
3. Have student wear headsets to muffle noise
4. Seat child away from doors/windows
5. Seat child near model (parent teacher or peer/sibling)
6. Vary working surface (e.g., floor or vertical surface)
7. Simplify/shorten/amplify directions
8. Give both oral and written directions
9. Have student repeat directions
10. Have student repeat lesson objective
11. Change cognitive/difficulty level of question
12. Change response format (e.g., written to spoken)
13. Provide sequential directions
14. Use manipulatives/concrete materials
15. Alter expected objective criterion/proficiency level
16. Reduce number of items on assignments/tests
17. Highlight relevant/key words, phrases, and features
18. Use rebus (i.e., picture) directions
19. Provide more practice trials
20. Increase allocated time
21. Develop/teach a step-by-step strategy for the task
22. Change type of reinforcer (e.g., edible, tangible, activity, etc.)
23. Increase amount of reinforcer given at one time
24. Increase number of times child receives reinforcer
25. Delay reinforcement
26. Increase response wait-time after a question
27. Use specific rather than general praise
28. Have peer/sibling serve as tutor/checker
29. Provide frequent review
30. Have student summarize at end of lesson
31. Use self-correcting materials
32. Adapt test items for differing response modes
33. Provide mnemonic devices
34. Provide tangible reinforcers
35. Establish routines for handing in work, etc.
36. Use timers to show allocated time
37. Provide visual cues (e.g., posters, banners, etc.)
38. Block out extraneous stimuli on written material
39. Tape record directions
40. Tape record student responses
41. Use a study guide
42. Provide critical vocabulary list for content material
43. Provide essential math fact list during math assignments

44. Use clock faces to show classroom routine times
45. Use dotted lines to line-up math problems or show margins
46. Provide transition directions between adjacent activities
47. Assign only one task at a time
48. Provide discussion questions before reading/assignments
49. Use word markers to guide reading lines of text
50. Alter sequence of presentation
51. Enlarge/highlight key words on test items
52. Provide daily/weekly assignment sheets
53. Post daily/weekly schedule
54. Use graph paper for place value or during computation of digits
55. Establish rules and review frequently
56. Teach key directions words (e.g., circle, underline, define, etc.)
57. Allow student to use a pencil grip
58. Tape assignment paper to desk surface
59. Shorten project assignments in daily tasks
60. Break directions down into segments
61. Number/order assignments to be completed
62. Place student's desk closer to black/white board
63. Incorporate wholesome, currently popular themes/characters into lessons
64. Repeat major points in a lesson before concluding
65. Use verbal cues while speaking (e.g., "One...two...," "Don't write this down.")
66. Pause appropriately after emphasis points during teaching
67. Change tone of voice (e.g., loud to whisper) and inflection (e.g., high to low)
68. Collect notebooks periodically to review/check accuracy/notetaking skills
69. Reorganize tests so that items progress from easy to hard
70. Color code place value tasks
71. Use self-teaching materials
72. Do only odd/even numbered items on long assignments/worksheets
73. Use a typewriter/word processor/computer
74. Provide organizers (e.g., cartons, bins) for desk materials
75. Teach student scanning/skimming skills for varied reading rates
76. Provide written summaries of content taught during lesson
77. Use peer-mediated teaching/strategies (e.g., buddy system)
78. Call student's name before asking a question
79. Use extra line spaces between lines of text
80. Color code materials/directions
81. Provide calculators for higher order mathematics
82. Circle math computation sign
83. Use hand signals to cue behavior (e.g., attention, responding)

Adapted from *Instructional Modification Menu* (pp. 201-203) by S. Cohen, 1993, *Effective Instruction: Principles and Strategies for Programs*, in B. S. Billingsley (Ed.), *Program Leadership for Serving Students with Disabilities*, Richmond, VA: Virginia Department of Education. Reprinted by permission.

dations for students in the areas of test-taking and completing assignments:

Test-taking. One or more of the following variables may need to be altered when students with learning difficulties take daily tests in home school:

- Test administration
- Number of test items
- Mode of response to test items

Tests traditionally are given to students in written form. But teachers make a number of assumptions when giving written tests to students. Some teachers assume that children have adequate vision, visual processing skills, and reading decoding skills, to mention a few. But some struggling learners have limitations in one or more of these areas. Thus, it is not only appropriate, but necessary for tests be modified to meet their needs. For example, it may be that the home teacher would need to read the items orally to the child or possibly even administer the test on computer rather than on paper for a multisensory effect and/or to increase the child's motivation.

The parent could also dictate the test items on a tape recorder, and the child could pause, rewind, and replay as needed. The more direct application of audiotaped tests may be in heritage studies, geography, and science where understanding and mastery of content is the goal, not demonstration of decoding or comprehension skills per se. For example, if the child has a learning disability in reading, then giving him a science test in written format may not allow him to show what he has learned. He probably won't get past the barrier of having to read the questions on the test. In order to compensate for having to press/release recorder keys (i.e., "pause", "rewind", etc.) on the tape player, parents should allow students extra time to complete audiotaped tests.

The number of test items can also be modified. For example, a child is due for a unit test on adding three-digit numbers with and without regrouping. A typical test may include 10 problems on addition with no regrouping and 10 problems on addition with regrouping for a total of 20 problems. For typical learning disabled students, however, a math test with 20 problems may take an inordinate amount of time for them to complete. However, altering the test to include only 5-7 of each of the two types of addition problems for a total of 10 to 14 problems would accommodate for the reduced attention spans that many learning disabled students have. Despite the fact that there are fewer questions on the test, you will still get an adequate sampling of their learning.

Finally, you can alter how the student responds to test questions. Many educators, both in conventional and home schools alike, place too much emphasis on written responses. It may surprise some parents to know that there is nothing etched in stone, theoretically speaking, that says students must provide written responses to test questions. Conventional educators typically require written test responses many times to facilitate large groups of students in their classrooms. Recognizing, however, that struggling learners may have certain limitations that prevent them from responding in written form, parents may have to obtain their answers to test questions in different ways. If we allow these students to speak their answers out loud, or dictate them on audiotape, or key them into a computer, we are allowing them to work around their writing barrier so they can show what they have learned.

We must be ever aware of our primary goal in giving tests. For example, the goal of science and history tests is to measure the student's mastery of content-specific skills that we have taught them and not to determine whether he is adept at the underlying processes or mechanics of test-taking (i.e., reading decoding and handwriting responses). Making the modifications we have recommended above for test-taking should preserve the academic integrity that we are striving for, yet allow the struggling learner to show that he has mastered the expected material. We believe it is important that parents make written notation on the test as to the specific modifications that were allowed the student for documentation purposes.

Assignment Completion. Struggling learners, as with other typical learners, will have various assignments that they must complete including seat work, homework, projects, and so on, many of which may involve writing in some sort or fashion. Parents may need to provide one or more of the following accommodations to assist struggling learners in successfully completing their assignments:

- Give extended time to complete work
- Allow oral presentation of assignments
- Accept dictated, audiotaped work
- Allow use of a computer/typewriter

Modifying With A Tape Recorder

Integrating a simple piece of technology—the audiotape recorder—into the instructional blueprint for struggling learners in the home school should increase the likelihood that they will succeed.[15] What follows are ideas on how home teachers can modify instruction using audiotape recorders in reading, writing, and spelling activities.

Reading. Struggling learners typically have difficulties in reading decoding and comprehension. Try audiotaping textbook chapters for them to use as they read. Audiotaping textbooks can be a laborious project, but securing and organizing volunteer readers (e.g., older siblings in the household, grandparents, home educating neighbors, church members) can greatly reduce the parent's burden. C. Mercer and A. Mercer[16] offer these guidelines in preparing audiotapes:

- Tape in a fully-furnished room to absorb noises
- Turn the volume low before recording to avoid clicks on the tape
- Fade the volume before stopping
- Vary readers to reduce boredom
- Identify chapter titles/page numbers at the beginning
- Ring a bell to signal the end of a page
- Pause at paragraph divisions to allow for absorption
- Record a brief beginning message instructing the student to listen properly, to stop to take notes occasionally, and to turn the page at the bell.

Students should always use headphones and follow the printed text visually as they receive auditory support from the tapes. This encourages active learning and allows for greater content absorption.

Parents may want to consider securing ready-made audiotaped textbooks from Recordings for the Blind (RFB). This organization will provide audiotapes for any textbook upon request. If they do not have tapes for a certain book, you need only notify RFB in advance and they will prepare the tapes at no charge. RFB does require a nominal one-time fee (less than $40) and a special tape player must be purchased or leased in order to use the tapes (See Appendix A).

Writing. Use the tape recorder as a medium for students who have difficulties getting thoughts from their heads to paper. Have the student develop a rough outline (2-3 major points with 2-3 subpoints) of the topic he will be writing about. Using the major points and subpoints, the student will then dictate his thoughts (in complete sentences) on to the tape recorder. The student should avoid dictating his entire paper in one sitting. Encourage him to focus on one major point at a time. Once the entire paper has been recorded on tape, the home teacher can then assist the student in transcribing the dictated material via typewriter or computer word processing as well as help the student in error monitoring for corrections before turning the paper in to be graded.

Spelling. Struggling learners can also be taught how to use the tape recorder for studying/preparation and testing in spelling. The student should record his spelling words on tape as a first step (leaving a 5-second pause between each word). The student can then administer practice tests to himself at home. Using headphones will help block out interfering noises. The student should be instructed to use the "pause" or "stop" buttons to allow more time for processing and the actual written production of the word to be spelled. The parent should allow the student to use the spelling word tapes during class time for use on the final spelling tests. The student can self-administer his spelling test via audiotape (with headphones).

Once more, we recommend that parents keep a record of the types of instructional modifications and accommodations that they are allowing their children. For example, it would be wise to note on the first page of a science test that the student was allowed to speak his answers, or that the test items were dictated to him, and so on. As we will address in greater detail in Chapter 11, this is part of the necessary documentation that parents of struggling learners must be careful to keep on the child.

---

[1]J. Sutton (1993c)
[2]Nowacek, McKinney, & Hallahan (1990)
[3]J. Sutton, McKinney, & Hallahan (1992)
[4]Englert (1983)
[5]Englert (1984)
[6]Englert & Thomas (1982)
[7]Haynes & Jenkins (1986)
[8]Kaufman, Agard, & Semmel (1985)
[9]Leinhardt, Zigmond, & Cooley (1981)
[10]Sindelar, Smith, Harriman, Hale, & Wilson (1986)
[11]Fouse & Brians (1993), p. 29
[12]Cohen (1993)
[13]Nelson & Lingnugaris-Kraft (1989)
[14]Bursuck, Rose, Cowen, & Yahaya (1989)
[15]J. Sutton & C. Sutton (1994)
[16]C. Mercer & A. Mercer (1989)

GENERIC TEACHING TECHNIQUES

M odifying instruction may be enough to help some strug gling learners succeed academically and behaviorally. For others, though, and particularly for those with bona fide forms of disability that adversely affect their learning, the parent may need to employ one or more specialized teaching methods during times of regular or remedial instruction in order for the child to realize success. From our reading of the literature and experience, we have identified a number of teaching methods that can be easily implemented by parents.

We open this chapter with a discussion of general teaching techniques that parents will want to consider implementing on a daily basis for struggling learners. We then concentrate on specific teaching techniques that can be used with just about any subject, from reading to mathematics. We close the chapter with some ideas that parents can use with students who have memory difficulties.

General Teaching Techniques

Giving instructions are an integral part of any teacher's daily teaching routine. Although teachers of typical learners many times resort to an almost conversational, non-deliberate style of giving instructions, parents of children with learning difficulties will often find this style ineffective. Not only are struggling learners' listening and attention skills noticeably weaker, but they also process information with greater difficulty (note discussion of processing difficulties of LD students in Chapter 2). Parents, therefore, will need to employ a more intentional, more deliberate means of delivering instructions to these students before they approach learning tasks.

The Council for Exceptional Children,[1] the leading professional organization for special educators, recommends the following ideas to teachers who work with ADD students (we believe these suggestions are applicable to any type of struggling learner):

- Use more than one modality [e.g., visual, auditory, etc.] when giving directions.
- Use alert cues [e.g., say, "Eyes right here..."] to get attention before giving directions

Garnett[2] gives these additional recommendations, which are directed to teachers of ADD students. Again, we believe these ideas generalize to virtually any student with learning difficulties:

- Ensure a good amount of eye contact when giving verbal instructions.
- Make directions clear and concise. Simplify, when needed.
- Be CONSISTENT with daily instructions.
- Be sure the youngster comprehends *before* beginning the task. Have him/her repeat instructions *in words* [aloud back to the teacher].
- If you need to repeat, do so with the understanding that it is legitimately needed. Remember, being clear, kind and firm is a model for how the youngster will treat *himself* and others.
- Help the youngster learn to seek help appropriately (many children...will not ask).
- Provide the structure of a daily assignment book, monitoring the accuracy of what gets written in it [i.e., the actual assignment pages, number of problems, etc.]...

You may wish to concentrate on incorporating just one of these ideas per week rather than tackling them all at once. Gradually working in these teaching techniques one at a time will allow you ample time to perfect one before adding in another. It also allows the student the necessary time he needs to adjust to slight changes in how you instructionally interact with him rather than being bombarded with all of them at one time. Parents of struggling learners who implement these ideas gradually and enforce them consistently will see a noticeable change in the academic performance of their child in the long-run. These general teaching techniques used alone may not be enough for some children with learning difficulties. One or more of the remaining teaching techniques that follow may also need to be employed by the home teacher.

Specific Teaching Techniques

We describe and illustrate the following teaching techniques in this section: direct instruction, Cloze technique, strategy training, self-monitoring, musical mnemonics, and computer-assisted instruction. Our experience has been that these particular methods can be applied to the teaching of various subjects including reading, spelling, writing and mathematics.

Direct Instruction

Direct instruction has also been characterized as *active teaching*.[3] Good describes the active teacher as one who provides brief presentations and demonstrations of information and concepts. The teacher also provides feedback to student recitations and questions as well as follow-up assignments that include instructions and practice examples. Monitoring of student progress is important in active teaching, and the teacher gives additional feedback and reteaches when necessary.

Direct instruction is a teaching method that can be used successfully in teaching virtually any subject area where the student is required to master academic performance skills, which would include reading, mathematics, science, and social studies. Commercially-produced direct instruction programs are available, for example, *Reading Mastery: DISTAR Reading*[4] and *DISTAR Arithmetic I, II, and III*.[5,6,7] The teaching parent may find, however, that the direct instruction procedure discussed by Becker, Engelmann, and Thomas[8] will more than sufficiently serve their purpose in teaching the struggling learner at home without having to make the tremendous investment in purchasing the commercially packaged programs.

The Becker and associates'[9] model of direct instruction requires the teacher to incorporate the following nine carefully ordered steps in the teaching of new skills to the student:

(1) *Attention Signal*—Teacher calls student to attention by using a language/verbal cue such as, "Johnny...eyes on me!" or "David...look here!"

(2) *Task Stimulus*—Teacher presents task through use of a book, pictures, chalk/white board, easel, poster (e.g., a list of spelling/reading words on poster).

(3) *Stimulus-Direction*—Teacher instructs student to attend to the stimulus by saying words like "Look here..." or "Listen...please."

(4) *Stimulus-Prompt*—Teacher helps student attend to some specific characteristics of the stimulus by describing, expanding, or illustrating.

(5) *Response-Prompt*—Teacher helps student focus on <u>what</u> she will be asking or expecting the student to know in the question that follows; she specifies exactly what she expects the student to know.

(6) *Response-Direction*—Teacher questions the student and includes <u>how</u> the student will respond (i.e., verbal, written, or pointing).

(7) *Do-It Signal*—Teacher cues the student to respond; this is generally a perceptual cue, for example, a hand drop, tap on desk, finger snap, or it could be verbal (e.g., "Write your answer now.").

(8) *Task Response*—Student gives response to teacher's questions in verbal or written forms or by pointing (depending on what was indicated by the teacher in *Response-Direction*).

(9) *Reinforcer*—Teacher gives a social reinforcer (e.g., "Excellent!") along with one other type of reinforcer such as an edible (e.g., apple slices), tangible (e.g., stickers), or activity (e.g., two minutes of video game time) reinforcer.

We provide an example of teaching time skills using direct instruction in Figure 8.1. In a typical daily lesson, the teaching parent can expect to use direct instruction numerous times in teaching one or more single skills. It may be that the parent has to repeat the same teaching routine several times in succession for a child to understand. Yet the teacher can reteach the same skill using different examples and illustrations. Following the order of the direct instruction steps is critically important, so parents may need to practice and rehearse the procedure several times prior to the actual lesson that it will be used until it becomes automatic.

Figure 8.1

Direct Instruction
Clock Skills

Attention Signal:	"Jared...(tap on desk)...Look this way!"
Task Stimulus:	(Picture of clock face with 12 marks)
Stimulus-Direction:	"Look...(pointing)...at this clock."
Stimulus-Prompt:	"See...it has 12 marks. You remember last week we learned that each hour of the day has 60 minutes."
Response-Prompt:	"Well...each mark here represents 5 minutes out of a 60-minute hour."
Response-Direction:	"On a scrap piece of paper, write the number of minutes that each mark stands for on this clock."
Do-It Signal:	"Do it now."
Task Response:	(Jared writes the number "5" on scrap paper.)
Reinforcer:	"Terrific!" (Mother gives Jared a token point.)

Cloze Technique

The Cloze technique[10] has been promoted primarily as an informal assessment tool for use with students who have reading comprehension difficulties.[11] Luftig[12] describes how this technique works:

> This technique involves selecting passages of approximately 260-275 words of varying degrees of difficulty. Words are then deleted from the passages and the child is asked to write in the missing words. In order to write in these missing words, the child needs to glean contextual clues from the surrounding words and sentences in the passage. The logic is that the ability to glean such contextual meaning from surrounding phrases is a sign of reading comprehension.

Levey,[13] however, suggests that the Cloze technique can also be adapted for use in developing reading comprehension skills in children. She recommends that teachers follow these steps in constructing reading comprehension activities for students who add/omit words during reading or who are whole-word readers:

(1) Choose a passage of 100 words at the child's functioning reading level;

(2) Leave the first and last sentences in tact, but for all sentences in-between, leave every fifth or tenth word blank;

(3) Provide the list of missing words that corresponds *in correct order* with the blanks in the reading passage;

(4) Have the student read the passage and place the words from the list on the blanks;

(5) Once mastery has been achieved with this format, construct additional passages, but provide a list of missing words *in mixed order* from which the student may choose;

(6) Succeeding word lists should include only selected words [not all missing words] in mixed order, which forces the student to use contextual clues to determine remaining missing words;

We believe the Cloze technique can be further adapted for use in teaching mathematics skills. Consider the following example of solving linear equations (list of missing elements are provided in order for the student to fill-in):

<u>Fill-In List</u>

$$5x - 9 = 2x + 3$$
$$-2x \quad -\square \qquad\qquad 2x$$

$$\square - 9 = 0x + \square \qquad 3x, 3$$
$$3x + \square = \quad + 9 \qquad\qquad 9$$

$$3x = \square \qquad\qquad 12$$

$$\underline{3x = 12}$$
$$\square \quad 3 \qquad\qquad 3$$

$$x = \square \qquad\qquad 4$$

Strategy Training

Responsible, independent adults use step-by-step strategies on a regular basis to solve many of their routine, day-to-day tasks and problems. For example, a mother goes through several steps in her mind in accomplishing the task of grocery shopping: (1) Are the kids coming or no? (2) Do I have my shopping list? (3) Do I have the checkbook or cash? (4) How will I get to the store—car, truck, etc.? and so on. Thus, our suggesting that strategy training be used as a special method to teach students with learning difficulties should be no surprise to parents. Using strategies is simply a normal part of life. Many parents make the assumption that children already have strategies to accomplish learning tasks. Although some average learners do demonstrate good strategies and know when to use them, students with learning difficulties generally do not. Parents, therefore, will need to teach strategies directly and intentionally to struggling learners in order for them to be strategy efficient.

Deshler, one of the leading scholars in the field of strategy instruction, has defined *learning strategies* as "techniques, principles, or rules that enable a student to learn, solve problems, and complete tasks independently."[14] There are many different types of learning strategies that children will need to be taught (e.g., organization, study, review, memory, assignment completion, time management, and test-taking strategies). Learning strategies "can be used in all content areas, as well as for developing appropriate social skills."[15] More important, learning strategies help students learn *how* to learn.

A number of learning strategies have been developed by various researchers. Consider, for example, COPS, an error-monitoring strategy for writing by Ellis and Lenz.[16] Each letter in the mnemonic prompts the student to check his writing for a specific type of error before turning in his paper to be graded by the teacher:

C = Have I capitalized the first word and all proper nouns?
O = How is the overall appearance?
P = Have I used end punctuation, commas, and semicolons correctly?
S = Do the words look like they are spelled right...?

The COPS strategy would be applicable to any subject where the student would be required to do a written assignment, not just English classes.

Robinson[17] developed an assignment completion strategy, AWARE, that requires the student to set goals and self-evaluate his performance. The strategy requires the student to record his responses to self-evaluation questions on a grid, like the one below:

ASSIGNMENT	A	W	A	R	E
1					
2					
3					
4					

Robinson[18] defines each of the letters in the mnemonic as follows:

A = Ask yourself what grade you want to earn [i.e., A, B, etc, or 100%, 90%, etc.]. Put the score in the box labeled A.

W = WORK-Note...how much time you think it will take to complete the assignment.

A = Assignment completed? Check yes or no.

R = Rate your effort. What score do you think your teacher will give you?

E = End result. What score did you receive?

The student's responses to "A" and "W" are recorded on the grid prior to beginning the assignment or project. The next two items, "A" and "R," are recorded on the grid by the student immediately after completion of the assignment. The final item, "E," is recorded after the teacher grades the assignment. The parent should discuss with their child any discrepancies between the child's self-evaluation (i.e., his ratings for "A," "W," "A," and "R") and the parent evaluation (i.e., "E").

Carman and Adams[19] developed a test-taking strategy, SCORER, that is taught and used universally by special educators. SCORER should be used primarily when taking objective-type tests (i.e., multiple choice, true/false, etc. items). Each letter in SCORER cues the student to remember an important test-taking principle:

S = Schedule your time.

C = Look for clue words.

O = Omit difficult questions [i.e., postpone until later].

R = Read carefully.

E = Estimate your answers.

R = Review your work [making sure not to forget omitted items].

I recently recognized first-hand the value of learning strategies when preparing for a test that was required in order to secure a professional license. One of the requirements was to demonstrate mastery of basic elements of the U.S. Constitution. In order to organize the material so that it could be learned more efficiently, I formed various mnemonics or acrostics. For example, one of the questions in the study guide was as follows: By what means has the Constitution been changed since its adoption? The answer—by amendment, court decisions, and presidential practices. The mnemonic CAP ("C" for court decisions; "A" for amendment; "P" for presidential practices) was formed.

In like manner, parents can design strategies for their children at any time and for any learning task that they determine a need. But strategies don't always have to be in the form of an acrostic. They can be as simple as breaking a learning task down into its sequential steps, listing them on an index card, and having the child check off the steps of the strategy as he completes them. Fouse and Brians[20] describe the process of developing and teaching a strategy as follows:

> In strategy instruction the teacher first determines the curriculum [or task] demands with which the student is having difficulty and then matches a learning strategy to meet the specific demands. In teaching the strategy, the instructor determines the student's current learning habits and then describes and models the new learning strategy. The student should verbally rehearse the strategy and practice with controlled materials [i.e., hand-selected by the teacher and done under the teacher's observation and supervision] followed by classroom materials. The teacher then evaluates to determine student mastery of the strategy.

A critical step in teaching a strategy is that the parent should talk with the student and make sure that he understands the inefficiency of his previous way of approaching and solving a learning task. Getting a student to this point may require a series of one-on-one conferences/discussions. The parent may even need to review with the student (preferably in private) some samples of his/her tests, papers, worksheets, etc. that illustrate the inefficiency of the student's former way of accomplishing a task. Until the student recognizes that his way of accomplishing a task is indeed inefficient, then he will probably not be willing to accept a new learning strategy to replace the old one. As with teaching almost any new skill to a child (e.g., rollerskating, bike riding), parents will need to be patient with themselves and with the child in this phase of strategy training, recognizing that some students may need additional explanations and reminders of their inefficient way of solving tasks.

Also, parents must not underestimate the importance of modeling the strategy for the student before expecting the student to perform it independently. Modeling, of course, is greatly emphasized in Scripture, both directly and indirectly. The Lord Jesus Himself came to this world to provide a way of salvation for sinful man and to model a godly life for us. The written Word of God presents various models of men and women who loved God and served Him with all their might. Biblical models were provided so that we might imitate and incorporate in our lives the same principles of character and Christlikeness. So it is when modeling is applied to strategy instruction. Parents must sufficiently model the strategy for the child prior to holding the child responsible for using the strategy in learning tasks.

Self-Monitoring

Many struggling learners, particularly learning disabled and attention deficit disordered students, typically have problems in coming to and/or maintaining attention and remaining on-task . Drug therapy and the use of psycho-stimulant drugs such as Ritalin, Cimetidine, Dexedrine, etc. remain, nonetheless, one of the most popular treatments for children with severe attentional problems. Our view is that parents would be wise to consider drug treatment only as a last resort after other non-drug approaches have been exhausted and perhaps only for the most severe cases of inattention.[21] We agree with Strayer[22] who holds that, "[The] use of drugs with our children...[is] not a first or third or fourth choice of treatment. It comes about last on the list..."

Although taking a drug for attentional problems is easy and convenient for both parents and child, the research on its effectiveness is presently inconclusive. For example, Swanson and his colleagues[23] have reviewed available studies and concluded that use of psycho-stimulant medication produces only *temporary* management and improvement of behavior problems typically associated with attention deficit disorder. More important, drug therapy generally results in "frequent problems with eating and sleeping" with "no significant improvement in reading skills...athletic or game skills...positive social skills...[and] no improvement in academic achievement."[24]

We also agree with Short[25] that children with attentional difficulties "[do] not have to be treated with drugs as many school children are." Drug therapy is not the only approach that can be used to help children who have attentional problems. Other inexpensive, non-pharmacological approaches have been found to be effective. For example, a technique called "self-monitoring" will equip children with the skills they need to regulate and evaluate their own behavior. Hallahan and his colleagues[26] have concluded that self-monitoring "works best when attention is the primary problem." We believe that teaching a child to monitor his own behavior is an ultimate goal of every Christian parent and teacher. In addition to helping a child control his attention, self-monitoring should assist children, once they become adults, in being independent in many life skills and behaviors.

Self-monitoring for attention is a technique that makes use of a continuous-play audiotape with random tones/beeps that helps a child stay on-task during class time, seatwork or independent study without continual intervention by the parent. This technique can also be used to help children attend better to the parent's voice. Using an earphone or headphone set and a standard tape player, the child is cued audibly by beeps on the tape, which occur randomly at 15- to 120-second intervals. At each beep, the child asks himself, "Was I paying attention to my work (or the teacher)?" The child then marks either "yes" or "no" on an accompanying check sheet. Wrist counters, print-out-style calculators, and grocery counters can also be used as recording instruments. Parents will need to train their youngster in self-questioning and in using the self-monitoring tape.

It is important in self-monitoring to set an attention goal for the child. The initial goal can be established by calculating the average of the percentages of "yes" responses on the first week's worth of check sheets. The "yes" goal can then be increased gradually across school weeks. Parents may increase the power of this technique by issuing appropriate rewards and reinforcers[27] contingent upon the student meeting the pre-determined success goal.

It might be good to use self-monitoring sparingly in the beginning. This technique is highly structured and students may resist having to account for their attention so frequently. There may be less resistance, however, if parents carefully choose reinforcers/ rewards that the child strongly desires (please refer to Chapter 10 on how to select appropriate reinforcers/rewards for children). Once a child's attention span has increased to an acceptable level using self-monitoring, the various elements of the technique can be faded or weaned away, one at a time (the audiotape first, then the check sheet/recording device). Reintroduce either or both of these two elements when attention skills show signs of waning.

Parents can make their own self-monitoring audiotape for use in the home or purchase an inexpensive commercially-produced version developed by Dr. Harvey Parker[28] which is available from the ADD Warehouse in Florida. Dr. Parker's kit includes the audiotape, a pack of check sheets, and an instruction manual and sells for approximately $20. A free catalog describing Parker's self-monitoring program, along with books and other non-drug products for children with attentional problems can be ordered by calling ADD Warehouse's toll-free number (see Appendix A).

Musical Mnemonics

Most children, like adults, get much enjoyment from music. Music can also be relaxing. Dunlap[29] even recommends that parents listen to Baroque-style music in order to deal with the extra pain and stress that is brought on at times when home educating struggling learners. But music is more than just a means of relaxation or source of aesthetic pleasure. In short, it can be used to help people accomplish their work. It is not unusual to hear someone humming or whistling a tune as they are working. Many businesses will play music for their customers or clients (e.g., department stores, grocery stores, physician's office, etc.) while services are being delivered. Some employers use music to maximize the work performance of their employees (e.g., assembly lines). In an educational sense, we know that music can be used to assist students in learning and remembering subject matter information.

The ability for a child to recall and remember information accurately is one indicator that effective learning has occurred. This is what a mnemonic is designed to accomplish. But the use of mnemonics in teaching is not a novel idea. I can still remember back to my early grade school years when I sat next to my grandmother on the piano bench for lessons. Like many other piano teachers, she employed mnemonics to teach the various key positions in the bass and treble clefs. For example, the word, "FACE" helped me remember each of the treble notes in the spaces on the treble clef, since the notes were in the order, F-A-C-E, as you read from the bottom to the top of the staff.

Gfeller[30] reviewed available studies that investigated the effectiveness of *musical mnemonics* with retarded/slow children and found that theorists have concluded that the "heightened attention and the optimal balance of redundancy and novelty in musical stimuli contribute to improved recall of information." From a practical perspective, we know this to be true. Very few of us who came from functional homes with caring, loving parents escaped learning the traditional ABC jingle. In our work with disabled students, we have always found it interesting that even those with very low ability (i.e., IQs in the retardation range) can recite the ABC song with just as much fluency as children with normal to above normal ability.

Gfeller states that musical mnemonics can be used when teaching learning tasks that reflect factual information (e.g., math facts, states and capitals), procedural steps/rules (e.g., grammar rules), and motoric activities when self-monitoring is needed (e.g., constructing letters during writing). Gfeller[31] further adds that it is important to choose a familiar tune, if possible, on which to construct the mnemonic and that, once developed, it should be "demonstrated, practiced, and finally reinforced" with the child. Parents may wish to follow these steps in developing and teaching musical mnemonics:

(1) Select a tune;
(2) Apply the lyrics [i.e., the desired skill];

(3) Model the musical mnemonic several times for the child;

(4) Have the student sing along with you [reinforce promptly];

(5) Have the student sing the mnemonic alone [reinforce promptly];

(6) Have the student gradually fade from singing overtly, to humming, to using an "inner voice" [reinforce promptly]; and

(7) Monitor child's application of the mnemonic [reinforce promptly].

Computer-Assisted Instruction

Many children are dazzled at the various computerized toys that are on the market today. It seems that, when nothing else will capture a child's attention, a computer can. We are convinced that the teaching parent who works with a struggling learner should capitalize on the computer's capability to motivate children to learn. There are a number of specific instructional benefits when parents use computers in teaching children with learning difficulties:

• Provides a multisensory approach to learning;

• Allows for a wide range of learning rates;

• Provides children with immediate feedback;

• Has the capability to record, store, and recall student responses; and

• Provides varied forms of positive reinforcement.

There are literally thousands of educational computer software programs on the market today, and choosing the right ones that are most effective from an instructional perspective can be difficult. Unfortunately, some computer programs can be considerably expensive. If parents don't choose wisely, they can unintentionally sink an entire school year's allocated money for instructional materials in useless software.

Although there are some educational software programs in the public domain realm that are useful with struggling learners, our experience has been that much of what is available is simply not sensitive to the unique needs of children with learning difficulties. One quarterly publication, *Special Times*, reviews hundreds of software titles from a wide variety of sources to determine which ones are most appropriate for children with learning disabilities.

The *Special Times*[32] review board believes that choosing software with the following eight characteristics will ultimately be most effective for struggling learners:

- Provides substantive (hopefully corrective) feedback to the student;
- Has an appropriate reading level that will not present a barrier to the student in absorbing/mastering the content of the program;
- Allows choices (e.g., picking content, different strategies, etc.);
- Does not require absolute correctness on first answers to questions, but allows the student several opportunities to get the correct answer;
- Does not limit the student on the amount of time to respond or the number of times to respond to questions;
- Allows the student to choose difficulty level;
- Has an attractive screen that is uncluttered and which does not distract the student from focusing on the learning task; and
- Has directions that are brief and optional and which do not cause the student to have to rely heavily on the teacher for assistance.

Parents can secure the *Special Times* magazine free by contacting Cambridge Development Laboratory, Inc. via letter or toll free number (see Appendix A). The magazine categorizes reviewed software in three areas: (1) language arts; (2) mathematics; and (3) essentials (i.e., gradebook programs, IEP programs, speech synthesizer programs, etc.). Prices begin around $29.95.

Techniques for Memorizing

In our work with home educating families, many have asked for ideas on how to help the struggling learner who has memory deficits. We do not believe, and have yet to see any proof (i.e., experimental studies) to the contrary, that some of the memory improvement programs being marketed today for exorbitant prices are effective with children who have learning difficulties. But we do believe that various techniques, if used consistently, can help children perform better on learning tasks that require them to recall and retrieve information that they have attempted to commit to memory.

The best collection of memory techniques that we are aware of has been compiled by Greenbaum.[33] Although these memory techniques were recommended in the context of memorizing for spelling, we believe these ideas can be generalized to memorizing other academic information that may be required of a child. Greenbaum suggests that memorization can be enhanced by:

- Saying/vocalizing the item to be memorized, but vary voice sound (e.g., from whispering, to shouting, to singing, etc.);
- Emphasizing/exaggerating vocally the difficult parts of the item to be memorized;
- Speaking the elements (e.g., letters, digits) while writing them;
- Highlighting with color the difficult parts;
- Underlining difficult parts;
- Varying the lettering font/style when writing difficult parts (e.g., switching from print to cursive, or choosing different letter font if using a computer/word processor);
- Varying the lettering size when writing difficult parts (e.g., switching from mix of upper and lower case to all upper case, or choosing different point type if using a word computer/ word processor);
- Using tactile letters/digits, but vary with difficult parts (e.g., switching from plastic/wood items to sandpaper);
- Varying writing surface and/or writing channel (e.g., chalkboard, whiteboard, manual typewriter, computer keyboard, writing in sand, writing on carpeting/floor); and
- Using finger tracing activities (e.g., over written words/ digits).

---

[1]CEC (1994), p. 11
[2]Garnett (1991), p. 4
[3]Good (1979)
[4]Engelmann & Bruner (1988)
[5]Engelmann & Carnine (1972)
[6]Engelmann & Carnine (1975)

[7]Engelmann & Carnine (1976)
[8]Becker, Engelmann & Thomas (1975)
[9]Becker, Engelmann & Thomas (1975)
[10]Taylor (1953)
[11]Luftig (1987)
[12]Luftig (1987), p. 177
[13]Levey (1984)
[14]cited in C. Mercer & A. Mercer (1989), p. 494
[15]Fouse & Brians (1993), p. 32
[16]Ellis & Lenz (1987)
[17]Robinson (1987)
[18]Robinson (1987), pp. 11-13
[19]Carman & Adams (1972)
[20]Fouse & Brians (1993), p. 32
[21]J. Sutton (1994d)
[22]Strayer (1994), p. 1
[23]Swanson, McBurnett, Wigal, Pfiffner, Lerner, M. A., Williams, Christian, Tamm, Willicutt, Crowley, Clevenger, Khouzam, Woo, Crinella, & Fisher (1993)
[24]Swanson et al. (1993), p. 159
[25]Short (1994), p. 39
[26]Hallahan, Hall, Ianna, Kneedler, Lloyd, Loper, & Reeve (1983), p. 104
[27]Parker (1992)
[28]Parker (1990)
[29]Dunlap (1994)
[30]Gfeller (1986), p. 28
[31]Gfeller (1986), p. 29
[32]Cambridge Development Laboratory, Inc. (1995, Spring)
[33]Greenbaum (1987)

TECHNIQUES FOR SPECIFIC SUBJECTS

While the methods we have discussed in Chapter 9 would be appropriate in teaching just about any subject, there are other techniques that are more appropriate for use with specific subjects. We present below key teaching methods that have been used by special educators across the country in teaching children with learning difficulties. The teaching parent will find these techniques both "user friendly" and easy to implement in the home for children who struggle with learning.

Reading Techniques

Probably the most prevalent area of learning difficulty among school-age children in America today is reading. Most parents recognize the critical importance of reading and the havoc it can reek on the lives of students who are poor readers, both for the present and the future. Not only is reading important for reading sake, but minimal reading skills are necessary if children are to absorb content in other subjects including science, history, and so on. More important still, the ability to read is an absolute requirement for a person to reach some semblance of success and independence in adult life. We have identified the following reading techniques as ones that can be easily implemented in homes by parents.

Multisensory/VAKT Method

It is generally believed by educators across the country that about 90% of classroom instruction is *visual* in nature, which suggests that students who are strong visual learners would stand to profit the most. For children with learning difficulties and who may learn better through auditory, kinesthetic (movement), and/or tactile (touch) means, a strong visual approach may be ineffective for the most part.

Therefore, the multisensory approach is designed to allow learners to input information from instruction using all four of the learning channels concurrently (i.e., visual, auditory, kinesthetic, and tactile); hence, the acronym VAKT is generally synonymous with multisensory instruction. Fichter[1] explains that, "With more senses actively involved in the learning process, there is a greater likelihood that the student will receive and process more information about the subject being taught" through multisensory instruction.

Dr. Grace Fernald,[2,3] one of the great special educators this century, is credited primarily with pioneering the multisensory approach. She used it as a remedial method with students who had serious learning problems, particularly in reading. The multisensory/VAKT approach is rightly a remedial teaching method that can be used in teaching whole-word reading (i.e., we would teach the word, "horse," as a whole word, not by its phonetic parts, "h-or-se"). A great advantage to this approach is that it allows poor readers the opportunity to build a basic reading vocabulary quickly. We believe that a balanced approach to teaching reading to struggling learners, though, will also include some phonics instructions along with VAKT reading instruction.

VAKT instruction has also been applied by some special educators to teaching spelling, vocabulary words, and arithmetic facts. The complete procedure for teaching a single word or math fact should take no more than two to five minutes. The parent will need the following materials:

- 3x11 inch strips of paper (typing paper cut three times the long way would work nicely);
- bold-colored markers or crayons that appeal to the child;
- 3x5 or 4x6 inch lined, index cards;
- index card box;
- lined notebook paper;

- pencils and pens; and
- computer and printer or typewriter.

C. Mercer and A. Mercer[4] describe the Fernald multisensory approach, which contains four stages that the student will gradually move through. The student should remain at the lower stage until he can show a high degree of mastery of words or math facts over a reasonable period of time. A synopsis of the stages follow:

1. The teacher writes the word or math fact on a paper strip. The student looks (visual) at the word or fact, while tracing (kinesthetic) the letters or numbers with his finger (touch) and listening to himself (auditory) pronounce or read it. The child repeats this process (perhaps up to a half dozen times) until he is ready to write the word or math fact on separate paper without looking at the strip. If he makes an error, he must go through the multisensory procedure for several more repetitions, and then attempt to write it again without error. Once the word/math fact is learned, the student records the word on an index card and files it alphabetically in the box (math facts are filed according to fact families (e.g., adding with 2s, multiplying by 5s, etc.). The student is then instructed to write a brief sentence or story using the word (or write a word problem using the math fact). The story (or word problem) is subsequently typed so that the student can see and read the word (or math fact) in print.

2. The teacher writes the word or math fact on a paper strip. At this stage, however, the student only looks (visual) at the word or math fact on the paper strip and pronounces/reads it (auditory) repetitively until he believes he has it mastered. He then writes it on separate paper correctly without error and files it accordingly in the card box. The student continues to write stories (or word problems).

3. The paper strips are removed at this stage, and the student learns the word or math fact directly from a piece of paper, as it is written (in manuscript or cursive). The students does no tracing or oral pronunciation or reading. The teacher is not required to write the word or math fact in this stage. The student may begin reading books at this stage, and the

teacher reviews continually words or math facts (filed previously).

4. The student needs no isolated printing of the word or math fact on separate paper and can "recognize new words by their similarity to printed words or parts of words already learned and thus can apply reading skills and expand reading interests."[5]

The multisensory approach remains very popular among special educators today and continues to be a widely used teaching approach in many remediation programs. However, Kavale and Forness[6] conclude that its effectiveness is inconclusive at this time. They indicate that some studies show that the multisensory approach produces positive results for some children, but it makes no significant difference in others.

Neurological Impress Method

The neurological impress method or NIM[7] is a remedial reading technique that may prove to be attractive to home teachers who are on a shoe-string budget, since the only instructional material required to implement this method is a reading book. C. Mercer and A. Mercer[8] describe this technique as "joint oral reading at a rapid pace by the student and the teacher...[which is]...based on the theory that a student can learn by hearing his own voice and someone else's voice jointly reading the same material." Using a reading book (as is, with no special preparation/alterations) that is on a level *slightly below* the student's present reading level, the home teacher can implement the NIM technique as follows:

The student is seated slightly in front of the teacher, and the teacher's voice is directed into the student's ear at a close range....The objective is simply to cover as many pages as possible in the allocated time, without tiring the student. At first, the teacher should read slightly louder and faster than the student, and the student should be encouraged to maintain the pace and not worry about mistakes. The teacher's finger slides to the location of the words as they are being read. As the student becomes capable of leading the oral reading, the teacher can speak more softly and read slightly slower, and the student's finger can point to the reading. Thus, the student and teacher alternate between leading and following.[9]

Home teachers should make sure that the learning environment is free from the noise and distractions of other children while using the NIM technique. Clearly, the NIM technique will give the struggling learner more experiences in reading decoding and oral reading rate than in comprehension per se. It may be wise, then, for the teaching parent to combine oral questions and discussion activities with the NIM technique in order to check for the student's comprehension and understanding of the material.

Computer-Assisted Reading Programs

As we discussed earlier, integrating computers in the daily instruction should yield great benefits for struggling learners in all subject areas, and reading is no exception. From our review of the reading computer software programs published in *Special Times*,[10] we recommend the titles listed in Figure 10.1. We caution Christian parents to screen these programs carefully, as some may have objectionable, non-Christian elements (e.g., wizardry, the underworld, etc.).

Spelling Techniques

Learning to spell proficiently presents major headaches for most students with mild forms of disability and for countless others with serious learning difficulties (not to mention their parents!). Little wonder this is so, for spelling requires a child to possess sufficient abilities in a number of cognitive skills such as visual imagery, visual memory, auditory discrimination and so on. Unfortunately, many, if not most, children with disabilities have major weakness in one or more of these cognitive skill areas.

Gordon, Vaughn, and Schumm[11] reviewed 17 research studies that investigated the effectiveness of various spelling interventions used by professional educators who taught LD students. They identified a number of teaching techniques that produced statistically significant increases in LD students' spelling performances. We discuss these in the paragraphs that follow.

Figure 10.1

Reading Computer Software

Title	Grade(s)	Vender	Computer(s)
Phonics Pinball	K-4	SWEPS Educ.	AP
Stickybear Reading	K-5	Optimum Resource	AP/IBM
Reader Rabbit 1,2,3	K-6	The Learning Co.	AP/IBM/MAC
Word Magic	2-6	Clearvue/SVE	AP
Reading Rodeo	K-4	Heartsoft	AP/IBM/MAC
Reading Fun	1-6	Troll Software	AP
Syllable Squares	3-12	Junior Software	AP
Treasure Drive: Reading...	3-12	Gamco	AP/IBM
Vocabulary Machine	1-12	Southwest/EdPsych.	AP/IBM
Word Launch	1-12	Teacher Support	AP/IBM/MAC
Word Attack Plus!	4-12	Davidson	AP/IBM/MAC
Developing Reading Power	4-7	Clearvue/SVE	AP
Word Munchers	1-5	MECC	AP/IBM/MAC
Back to the Story	1-8	Focus Media	AP
Stickybear/Comprehension	3-6	Optimum Resource	AP/IBM
Reading Comprehension	3-8	Heartsoft	AP/IBM/MAC

Error Imitation and Modeling

In teaching the student the correct spelling of a word, the parent should first reproduce in written form the student's misspelled rendition of the word. The parent can then model the correct spelling of the word, preferably on the line directly underneath the misspelled word. We suggest using graph paper (one letter per square), which will allow for vertical alignment of the letters between the misspelled and correctly spelled words. In a one-to-one correspondence manner, the child should be able to see more readily his error(s). You can emphasize the student's error(s) even more by using a colored pen to highlight vertically the corresponding pair(s) of missed and correct letter(s). Parents should continue to provide repeated presentations of error imitation followed by modeling on a single word until they are confident that the child fully understands.

Learning Fewer Words Per Day

Elementary spelling textbooks generally present 18 to 25 spelling words per lesson. The typical learner is expected to master one spelling "lesson" each school week. It is not unusual for conventional elementary teachers to pre-test the student on the entire spelling list for a given lesson early in the school week. The students then study and practice the whole set of spelling words until the final test is given near the end of the school week. Although many typical learners may know the majority of the spelling words at pre-test time and will, hence, have only a few words to master for the remainder of the week, it is just the opposite with struggling learners. They may perform poorly at pre-test time and be "overloaded" the remainder of the week with having to master virtually all of the words.

Our experience has been that a more incremental approach is necessary if children with learning difficulties are to succeed in spelling. That is, a designated number of words from the list must be directly taught and practiced each day until the entire list has been mastered. From their research on effective spelling interventions, Gordon and her colleagues[12] found that "overload and interference in spelling instruction" may be avoided if teachers present and expect students to learn no more than *three* spelling words per day. If home teachers abide by this recommendation and combine it with continuous review from one day to the next, then the child should be able to master approximately 15 spelling words per week.

Practicing Through Movement

Goldstein[13] has stated that, "What we do repeatedly we [will eventually] do automatically." Basketball coaches are notorious for making their players practice set plays over and over again prior to a game, so that the plays will be executed in a fluid, efficient manner during a game situation. This concept of repetitive practice is also applicable to the learning of various subjects, including spelling. Although some classroom teachers may argue to the contrary, researchers have concluded that having the child to practice spelling words through movement activities such as copying the word numerous times on paper, tracing templates or letter tiles, and even typing the word repeatedly on a conventional typewriter or computer keyboard increases spelling performance. In choosing a particular repetitive practice activity, it is important for teachers to "consider students' preferences [which are] likely to increase motivation to practice and learn."[14]

Spelling Strategies

We have already discussed the importance of strategy training (see Chapter 9) with children who have learning difficulties. Using strategies in the teaching of spelling is just one subject-area application of this concept. It is clear that, when students have an organized, systematic approach to learning spelling words, rather than just capriciously "looking" at the words as a way of trying to learn them, they do tend to be more successful. We believe that one of the best strategies to use is Stage 1 of Fernald's multisensory approach, discussed earlier in the reading section of this chapter. Parents should make sure that students follow the steps in order for Stage 1 when they attempt to learn spelling words.

Wong[15] believes that effective spelling instruction "appears to [require] two components: knowledge of phonics...and knowledge of spelling strategies." She developed a spelling strategy, which she tested in a study that involved eight sixth-grade students who qualified for remedial spelling instruction. Prior to the teaching of the spelling strategy, however, the teacher provided the following spelling instruction to each of the students:

- Pronunciation and meaning of words
- How to break words into syllables
- The structure of the words
- Decomposition of words into root word plus suffix (or prefix)
- Explanation of suffix (or prefix) concepts
- How words changed with the addition of suffix (or prefix)

Following this instruction, the teacher then taught the students the following *self-questioning* spelling strategy (a series of questions that the student was instructed to ask himself during the spelling test):

(1) Do I know this word?
(2) How many syllables do I hear in this word? [Write down the number.]
(3) I'll spell out the word.
(4) Do I have the right number of syllables down?
(5) If yes, is there any part of the word I'm not sure of the spelling? I'll underline that part and try spelling the word again.
(6) Now, does it look right to me? If it does, I'll leave it alone. If it still doesn't look right, I'll underline the part I'm not sure of the spelling and try again. [If the word I spelled does not have the right number of syllables, let me hear the word in my head again, and find the missing syllable. Then I'll go back to steps 5 and 6.]
(7) When I finish spelling, I tell myself I'm a good worker. I've tried hard at spelling.[16]

Wong reported that, prior to the teaching of the spelling strategy, the students could only demonstrate about a 30% spelling accuracy rate. Two weeks later, after the students had used the spelling strategy and were expected to demonstrate 100% mastery of a set of spelling words, a follow-up post-test showed that these students were still able to spell the words at almost an 80% accuracy level. Based on these results, it does appear that teaching a struggling learner to use this self-questioning spelling strategy may increase his spelling performance. The teaching parent should have little trouble adapting this strategy for use in the home.

Computer-Assisted Spelling Programs

We discussed in Chapter 9 some of the advantages and benefits of using computers as part of the instructional program for students with learning difficulties. Gordon and her colleagues[17] conclude from available research that "Computer lessons can enhance spelling performance and increase motivation to learn by capitalizing on students' interest." Based on our experience and review of spelling software programs for students in special education classes that have been recently published in the *Special Times* magazine (see Appendix A), we recommend the ones listed in Figure 10.2 for use in the home. Again, Christian parents are urged to check these programs carefully for objectionable elements.

Figure 10.2
Spelling Computer Software

Title	Grade(s)	Vender	Computer(s)
Crozzwords	3-12	Mindplay	AP/IBM/MAC
Lucky Seven Spelling...	3-12	Intellectual Soft.	AP/IBM
Spell It! Plus	5-12	Davidson	AP/IBM/MAC
Spelling Mastery	2-4	DLM/SRA	AP
Spelling Puzzles & Tests	K-12	MECC	AP
Spelling Rules	3-12	Optimum Resource	AP

Mathematics Techniques

Of all the academic subject areas, mathematics has received less attention by educators and researchers[18] with regard to identifying those remediation techniques and methods that work best with struggling learners. Moreover, little research exists to validate the effectiveness of the few techniques that are available for students with learning difficulties. Nonetheless, we believe that home teachers should be aware of several that can be easily implemented in the home setting for children who are struggling in mathematics.

Concrete-Pictorial-Symbolic Approach

Presenting information gradually from simple to complex is certainly a necessary and appropriate method of teaching of mathematics to children with learning difficulties. Many educators (e.g., C. Mercer & A. Mercer[19]) recommend the use of concrete objects or manipulatives in the early stages of teaching basic math skills. That young children need to be able to master touching and movement activities as part of their early learning experiences is a concept that is firmly grounded in Piaget's theory of cognitive development. Once children show mastery of a skill via concrete learning, then the teacher may gently lead them into pictorial learning experiences. The final stage of organizing and mastering knowledge would be at the abstract/symbolic level. The concrete-pictorial-symbolic teaching method, typically referred to as the "cognitive-developmental" approach, is one of the most important that parents could implement for children with learning difficulties.

We believe that students who continue to show delays in many basic math skills may never have been exposed sufficiently to concrete and/or pictorial teaching and learning in their early years. It is unfortunate that many mathematics textbooks begin instruction mostly at the abstract/symbolic level. Occasionally they will provide lessons with a pictorial learning emphasis, but rarely do you see the typical mathematics textbook commencing the teaching of a math skill at the concrete/manipulative level of learning. We recommend, therefore, that parents put careful thought into √ how the teaching of math skills can be developed through a series of methodical lessons that progress from the concrete to the pictorial to the abstract/symbolic levels of learning. This method of teaching will be especially critical when teaching older students who have gone years without demonstrating mastery of basic math skills. We illustrate by showing how a parent might teach place value using this approach.

Concrete Level. At the first level of learning, the teacher might secure several empty soup cans and, as a school activity, have the child decorate the cans using construction paper. The child should label each of four cans with the words, "Ones," "Tens," "Hundreds," and "Thousands." Each decorated can should be of a different color (e.g., Ones=red; Tens=blue; Hundreds=green; Thousands=orange) to help the student distinguish between them better. Several dozen popsicle sticks will also need to be purchased. The parent can then create several demonstration lessons where the student is taught how to group the sticks in bunches of ten, one hundred, etc. Continue grouping activities until the student can show mastery. The student is then taught how to place a representative stick in corresponding cans for groups of ten, one hundred, etc. Continue lessons of this sort until mastery occurs. The child shows complete mastery of the place value concept at the concrete level of learning when he can take a given set of popsicle sticks and place representative sticks in the appropriate corresponding place value cans with 100% mastery. Some students with learning difficulties may spend days or weeks at this learning level before they show 100% mastery.

Pictorial Level. Progressing to the pictorial level of learning, the parent would develop a series of worksheet activities (easy to do these days with computer graphics programs!) that would include pictures that represent the labeled place value soup cans and popsickle sticks that the student was touching and handling at the concrete level of learning. On these worksheet activities, the student would be expected to do with paper-and-pencil what he did in the concrete learning activities. One worksheet might include five different sets (quantities) of labeled popsicle tally marks along the left side of the worksheet, each with a corresponding set of four labeled soup cans along the right side of the worksheet.

The student would then be instructed to partition the groups of tally marks by circling smaller groups of ten, hundred, etc. and place a representative tally mark for each smaller group in the pictured soup cans. For example, if there were 34 tally sticks in one of the groups, then the student would circle three groups of ten, leaving four singles. He would then place one representative tally mark for each of the ten-groups, for a total of three, in the corresponding pictured "Ten" soup can, and four representative tally marks in the "One" soup can. Again, as with the concrete level of learning, parents should continue worksheet activities like this until the student can demonstrate 100% mastery.

Symbolic Level. Parents may want to use a fading procedure at this point as the student progresses from pictorial learning to abstract/symbolic learning. Once more, we suggest that parents develop a series of worksheet activities that require the student to continue circling groups of ten, one hundred, etc. popsicle tally marks. What would vary, though, is how the student writes/records the representative tally marks in the pictured place value soup cans. Worksheets should be constructed that gradually move from use of pictured soup cans to actual abstract symbols (i.e., digits and numbers). Consider presenting worksheets in the following order:

(1) tally marks in pictured, labeled soup cans;
(2) tally marks in labeled blanks instead of soup cans;
(3) digits (instead of tally marks) in labeled blanks;
(4) digits in unlabeled blanks; and
(5) digits alone without labels or blanks.

Alternative Math Strategies

Teaching mathematics to children has traditionally included many rule-driven, algorithms for solving math problems. For the most part, these algorithms are verbal in nature, using only words and including very few, if any, visual cues or prompts. Classroom teachers typically begin their instruction by demonstrating one or more sample problems, explaining as they go the sequential "steps" of the algorithm that the student must follow to solve the problem correctly. Students are then expected to memorize the steps.

Consider, for example, the following algorithm for adding fractions with unlike denominators typically taught by classroom teachers today:

Step 1: Find the least common denominator (which will require that the student do a second calculation on the side);

Step 2: Divide each given denominator into the new denominator (i.e., the least common denominator discovered in Step 1);

Step 3: Multiply each of these quotients times the corresponding given numerators for the new numerators.

Step 4: Add the two new numerators and bring over this sum for the numerator in the final answer.

Step 5: Bring over the least common denominator as the denominator in the final answer.

Step 6: Simplify.

Our experience has been that math algorithms like this one, although traditional, are difficult enough as it is for typical students who don't have learning difficulties. But for some struggling learners who have language and memory difficulties, however, these traditional algorithms are virtually impossible to master. In fact, many students with learning difficulties will go through most of their upper elementary and junior high school years, never mastering important basic math skills, but having nonetheless to endure teacher after teacher who presents the algorithm with little variety.

One of the best discoveries we made during our years as special education teachers was a number of "alternative" math strategies developed by experts in the field that were designed for students who have experienced little success learning math through conventional algorithms. These strategies are called "alternative" because they differ radically from the way math problems are traditionally solved. It has always been interesting yet mystifying to us that, after going through years of failure under traditional approaches, students with disabilities immediately gravitate toward alternative math strategies and will show success for the first time. We suspect that part of the reason why these strategies work with struggling learners has to do with a phenomenon to which Goldstein[20] was alluding when he said, "Sometimes the way to create change is to create a little confusion."

For example, Ruais[21] presents a low-stress, alternative math algorithm for adding and subtracting common fractions, which is called *Ray Multiplication* that requires only a few computations to reach a final answer. In addition, this strategy makes use of pictorial learning and cuing techniques. After learning the locational positions of the two numerators and two denominators, Ruais suggests that the student be taught to draw three rays (i.e., arrows): (1) from the lower left denominator [LLD] through the upper right numerator [URN]; (2) from the lower right denominator [LRD] through the upper left numerator [ULN]; and (3) from the lower left denominator [LLD] through the lower right denominator [LRD].

The student is then instructed to *multiply* the pairs of numbers that fall on the three rays and to write the products at the end of the arrowheads on the rays (See Figure 10.3). At this point, the student has everything he needs to complete the final answer, which has a final numerator and a final denominator. The final denominator is the product on the LLD/LRD ray (in our example, this would be 14). Depending on whether the problem is an addition or subtrac-

Figure 10.3

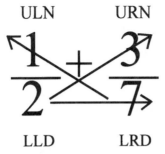

ULN   URN

LLD   LRD

tion problem, the final numerator is the sum or difference of the products on the LLD/URN and LRD/ULN rays. Since our example is addition, then the LLD/URN ray would be 6 and the LRD/ULN ray would be 7, which summed together would be 13. Thus, the final answer to this adding fraction problem would be 13/14. The student must then simplify his final fraction as necessary.

Another alternative math strategy called the *Combined Method* (author unknown) provides a different way to check columnar addition problems. The traditional approach to checking addition requires the student to add vertically in reverse (i.e., if the student adds vertically down the first time, then he will add vertically up for his check). Again, we have found that, for struggling learners with perceptual and directional problems, checking addition this way may be extremely troublesome.

In the *Combined Method*, the student is instructed first to add all of the digits of each addend in the problem, and to keep adding the digits in the resulting sums until only one digit remains for that addend (e.g., in 345, each digit is added, 3+4+5=12; then each digit in 12 is added, 1+2=3). Then, each of the resulting single digits from each corresponding addend are added and continue to be added until only one digit remains. The student will do the same "adding digits" process with the sum of the problem itself. The student then compares the two resulting single digits. If the two single digits are an exact match, then the original calculated sum is the correct answer. Conversely, if the two single digits are not equal, then the student made an error in calculating his original sum. An example of the *Combined Method* follows in Figure 10.4:

Figure 10.4

Combined Method

2 5 7 6   ☞ (add digits in addend) ☞ 20 ☞ (add digits) ☞ 2

5 1 5 2   ☞ (add digits in addend) ☞ 13 ☞ (add digits) ☞ 4

+3 8 4 0   ☞ (add digits in addend) ☞ 15 ☞ (add digits) ☞ 6

---

1 1 5 6 8 ☞   (add digits in sum) ☞ 21 ☞ (add digits) ☞ 3

In this example, the single digits that correspond with each of the addends continue to be added until the single digit, 3, remains (i.e., 2 + 4 + 6 = 12, and 1 + 2 = 3). Since this number, 3, is an equal match to the resulting 3 from the original sum, then we know that the calculated sum is indeed correct.

There are many other alternative math strategies. Since our space is limited, though, we refer our readers instead to a book co-authored by Reisman and Kauffman[22] entitled, *Teaching Mathematics to Children with Special Needs,* which may be more likely found at a university library (although local libraries could probably acquire the book through interlibrary loan). This publication contains numerous other alternative strategies like the ones we have discussed above.

Touch Math Program

The *Touch Math*[23] program is an increasingly popular, commercially-produced, multisensory math remediation program that is being used by conventional educators and private educational clinicians across the country. We believe this program would prove to be both cost effective and successful for parents in home schools who have children that demonstrate learning deficits in the skill areas of addition, subtraction, multiplication, division, number concepts, sequence counting, place value, and shapes and sizes. Bullock[24] describes the program as follows:

Touch Math is aptly named. It takes advantage of the very basic kinesthetic process of touching, plus counting. Each digit has a corresponding number of Touchpoints placed uniformly upon each character....With the digits 6 through 9, Touchpoints are grouped in twos when appropriate and differentiated graphically with a dot and a concentric circle. Single Touchpoints are touched and counted one time, while double Touchpoints are counted twice. Students are encouraged to count aloud and to follow a uniform touching/counting pattern.

Bullock[25] indicates that it takes first graders about a week to master the correct counting patterns using the *Touch Math* procedure, and that "Students introduced to *Touch Math* in later grades normally find it much easier than traditional methods." The program contains a variety of worksheet exercises and practice activities. Scott[26] tested the effectiveness of *Touch Math* recently with learning disabled and mentally retarded children and found that it produced significant gains for these children in the areas of addition and subtraction. See Appendix A for a mailing address and a toll-free number to contact for more information plus a free classroom sampler.

Hands-On Equations® Program

Developed and patented in 1986 by Dr. Henry Borenson, a nationally-known mathematics teacher, *Hands-On Equations*® [27] is also a commercially-produced, multisensory-form of instruction. This program introduces students to basic algebraic equations (e.g., $4x + 2 = 2x + 10$) by presenting various "hands-on" activities that follow the concrete, pictorial, and finally abstract/symbolic levels of learning. While requiring no prior knowledge of pre-algebraic skills (e.g., positive and negative numbers, etc.), *Hands-On Equations*® makes use of various game pieces which represent the different elements or terms of an algebraic equation that the student "balances" on a scale. Manipulatives include blue pawns (representing the x-variables), white pawns (representing inverse x's), red number cubes (representing positive integers), and green number cubes (representing negative integers). The scale, of course, represents the "=" in the equation.

Once the student learns how to translate the abstract/symbolic equation into its concrete counterparts, *Hands-On Equations*® gently leads the student through a series of 25 lessons that teach him how to make "legal moves," which allow the student to solve the equation physically, kinesthetically, and intuitively. In addition to providing students of any age with a sound introduction to algebra, other important features of the *Hands-On Equations*® program are that it, "brings success, enjoyment, and fascination to students...[and] enhances student interest in mathematics..."[28] Borenson reports that the program may be used as early as third grade with gifted students, fourth grade for average students, and fifth grade for learning disabled students. Borenson has recently developed a training video that should assist parents in understanding this technique. See Appendix A for more information.

Computer-Assisted Math Instruction

Again, we refer our readers to the *Special Times* magazine, which reviews and describes different computer software packages that are believed to encourage greater learning success in children who have serious learning needs. Many of the math programs include features which are educationally appropriate for use with learning disabled children and which parents can manipulate such as auditory/sound, speed/response time, difficulty levels, records of student progress, rewards and reinforcers (e.g., adventure games, printed certificates of excellence, etc.), test creation capability, diagnostic tests, and so forth. Although this list is not exhaustive, we have identified the mathematics computer programs listed in Figure 10.5 that we believe home teachers would find most useful.

In addition to the math techniques we have described above, home teachers may also be interested in a one-of-a-kind methods textbook used by some universities in preparing special education teachers to teach mathematics to learning disabled students. The book, *Teaching Mathematics to the Learning Disabled* (2nd ed.)[29] has numerous teaching techniques and strategies. Parents will find this book "user friendly" as it is not as research-oriented as many college textbooks. The book is available from Pro-Ed (see Appendix A). As we stated with the reading and spelling programs,

Christian parents will need to screen these math programs for objectionable elements.

Summary

Although we have presented some of the best and most effective teaching methods that can be used with struggling learners, the

---

Figure 10.5

Mathematics Computer Software

Title	Grade(s)	Vender	Computer(s)
Bake and Taste	1-9	Mindplay	AP/IBM/MAC
Comparison Kitchen	PreK-3	DLM	AP/IBM
Fraction Action	5-12	Unicorn	AP/IBM/MAC
Integers/Equations	5-10	Hartley	AP/IBM
Math Blaster Plus!	1-8	Davidson	AP/IBM/MAC
Math Concepts	2-8	Hartley	AP/IBM
Math Leap Frog	1-6	Gamco	AP/IBM/MAC
Math Word Problems	4-8	Optimum Res.	AP/IBM
Measure Works	2-6	MECC	AP
Millie's Math House	K-3	Edmark	IBM/MAC
Money	3-8	Gamco	AP/IBM
Place Value 1s,10s,...	3-6	EME	AP/IBM
Primary Word Math	K-5	Milliken	AP/IBM/MAC
Rounding	4-10	Gamco	AP/IBM
Stickybear Numbers	PreK-2	Optimum Res.	AP/IBM
Talking Clock	K-5	Orange Cherry	AP/IBM/MAC
The Coin Changer	K-6	Heartsoft	AP/IBM/MAC
The Calendar	2-8	Gamco	AP/IBM
Using a Calendar	3-6	Hartley	AP/IBM

---

teaching parent may still need more. There are a number of resource books available to assist parents in choosing additional teaching methods, many with little expense involved. Probably the premier teaching methods book on the market today for students with learning difficulties is one co-authored by Dr. Cecil Mercer and his wife, Ann Mercer, entitled, *Teaching Students with Learning Problems* (5th ed.).[30] It is typically used in special education methods courses for teachers in preparation, but it is, in our opinion, very readable and practical. The book is published by Merrill and contains almost 600 pages of information on teaching methodology for struggling learners and is organized by academic subject, that is, there are individual chapters on reading, writing, mathematics, etc. Bookstores should be able to special order this book directly from the publisher.

Appropriate teaching for children with learning difficulties entails not only knowing *how* but *what* to teach. This chapter has addressed *how* to teach. Deciding *what* to teach begins with having the child diagnostically tested to pinpoint specific skill deficits in the basic reading, writing, and mathematics areas (see Chapter 5 on Testing and Evaluation). These deficits many times represent prerequisite skills that the child has not mastered yet and which may be preventing him from learning more grade- and age-appropriate skills. An individualized educational plan (IEP, see Chapter 6) to remediate these deficit skills should then be developed prior to implementing the teaching techniques discussed above. Special education consultants can assist you in getting evaluators and planning individualized educational plans (see Chapter 7).

---

[1]Fichter (1993), p. 236
[2]Fernald (1943)
[3]Fernald (1988)
[4]C. Mercer & A. Mercer (1993)
[5]C. Mercer & A. Mercer (1993), p. 465
[6]Kavale & Forness (1987)
[7]Heckelman (1986)
[8]C. Mercer & A. Mercer (1993), p. 467
[9]C. Mercer & A. Mercer (1993), pp. 467-468
[10]Cambridge Development Laboratories, Inc. (1995, Spring)
[11]Gordon, Vaughn & Schumm (1993)
[12]Gordon, Vaughn & Schumm (1993), p. 178
[13]Goldstein (1989)
[14]Gordon, Vaughn & Schumm (1993), p. 179
[15]Wong (1986), p. 172
[16]Wong (1986), p. 172
[17]Gordon, Vaughn & Schumm (1993), p. 179
[18]Keller & J. Sutton (1992)
[19]C. Mercer & A. Mercer (1993)

[20]Goldstein (1989)
[21]Ruais (1978)
[22]Reisman & S. H. Kauffman (1980)
[23]Bullock (1994)
[24]Bullock (1992), p. 121
[25]Bullock (1992), p. 121
[26]Scott (1993)
[27]Borenson (1994)
[28]*The Hands-On Equations® Learning System* brochure
   (no date)
[29]Bley & Thornton (1995)
[30]C. Mercer & A. Mercer (1993)

Chapter

11

EDUCATIONAL PROCEDURES

M any classroom teachers will tell you that they routinely
follow certain educational procedures on a daily basis.
How the teacher gives tests to her students, grades their performance, and even schedules time for lessons are examples of educational procedures that should be automatic in a teacher's life as she
teaches and interacts with children from one day to the next. These
procedures add the structure that is necessary to make a school day
run smoothly. A more important benefit is that students can know
what to expect from their teacher and how to perform successfully
when certain educational procedures are consistently in force.

We have discussed a number of teaching techniques and
methods (see Chapters 8, 9, and 10) that parents should implement
in their child's educational program so that learning will be maximized. But we believe that a child's learning will be enhanced the
more and that parents of struggling learners will realize even
greater effectiveness if they develop and incorporate routine
educational procedures. This chapter, therefore, discusses and
illustrates a number of specific educational procedures that we
believe are appropriate for the teaching parent.

Basic Materials/Equipment

Home schools are characterized by their individualization and
flexibility. In fact, little is required for a parent to set up "shop"
(i.e., school), save a location and a child. Even the educational
materials used by home educators vary from one family to another.

But for parents of students with learning difficulties, we have found that certain basic materials and equipment are essential if routine educational procedures are to flow smoothly.

What follows is a list of basic teaching materials and equipment that are essential, particularly when the home instructional program includes a *remediation* component in combination with *regular* instruction. While it is understandable that many parents may not have the immediate funds to purchase all of these materials right away, they should probably begin purchasing items from this list on a regular basis until all have been purchased. Although this is certainly not an exhaustive list, many of these materials correspond with one or more of the teaching techniques discussed in Chapters 8, 9, and 10:

- Index cards (all sizes)
- Colored markers (water-based, bright colors)
- Manipulatives (popsicle sticks, plastic chips, marbles, etc.)
- Highlighter pens
- Pencil grips
- Construction paper (basic colors)
- Audiotape recorder/player (with built-in microphone and meter counter)
- Headphones for recorder/player
- Blank audiocassettes
- Solar calculator
- Portable study carrel (three-sided partition that will sit on the desk)
- Small writing board (white-type that uses markers)
- Computer (with color monitor and printer)

Classroom Arrangement

The location of the home classroom and the arrangement of furniture and materials are two important considerations in preparing a home classroom for teaching struggling learners. With regard to the location of the classroom, our experience has been that the teaching parent needs to be aware of a couple of things. One is that many, if not most, children with learning difficulties have attention and distractibility difficulties. And two, these children will need more frequent monitoring from the teaching parent than the other children in the household who may not have learning difficulties; hence, the classroom will need to be within close proximity for the parent.

We believe that, as much as is possible, the home classroom for struggling learners should be a separate room that has been set aside in the home for the sole purpose of education. At the same time, though, we recognize that the typical teaching parent will not own a mansion that has multiple floors of rooms just waiting to be occupied (really!). It may be that the home classroom will have to operate in another existing room that serves another purpose (e.g., dining room). For many mothers who find that they have to shuffle teaching responsibilities with other household duties, the dining room, in fact, may be the central-most location in the home and more easily accessible for most of the school day. It is our experience that two rooms in particular, the child's bedroom and the family room, can be very distracting and too "comfortable" for struggling learners. The teaching parent should probably steer clear of using either one of these rooms for the primary instructional setting.

With regard to furniture and equipment arrangement in the classroom, we recommend the floor plan in Figure 11.1, if you have a separate room in the home that can be designated soley for instruction. This layout allows for a separate storage closet, in

Figure 11.1

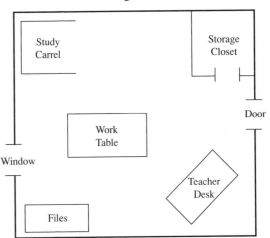

addition to file cabinets where more frequently used instructional materials can be stored and retrieved quickly. It also provides a central work place (i.e., the work table) where the teaching parent can work directly with the struggling learner on regular and remediation activities. The study carrel, where the student can concentrate on independent tasks, needs to be in a stimulus-free corner of the classroom and completely away from the "busier" parts of the classroom that may present distractions to the student.

Daily Schedule

Home instruction for students with learning difficulties should include a consistent daily schedule of activities. But developing a daily schedule that meets the unique needs of struggling learners can be complex and involved. Before a home teacher finalizes the daily schedule, it may be wise to answer a number of questions. For example:

(1) How much total time will be devoted to instruction each day?

(2) How much of the total daily instructional time will be allocated to *remedial* instruction?

(3) How much of the total daily instructional time will be allocated to *regular* instruction?

(4) How much time will be allocated to each individual subject lesson?

(5) How much of an individual subject lesson will be devoted to the "direct" teaching of a skill versus independent seat work?

(6) Which subjects need to be taught first or earlier in the day?

(7) How much time should be allocated to transition between lessons?

(8) How will the *remedial* lessons and the *regular* instruction lessons be arranged as far as order of presentation?

Getting answers to these questions will require that the parent consider the individual needs of the child. Since students with learning difficulties vary so much in their specific needs and abilities, it is virtually impossible for us to recommend "absolute" answers to these questions. Parents will also need to consider carefully the following additional questions as they begin to finalize the daily schedule:

(1) What is the child's maximum attention span in minutes, based on his ability to remain "on-task" and engaged in instruction once he comes to attention?

(2) What are the specific subject area(s) that are in most need of remediation and that may deserve more instructional minutes each day than others?

(3) Are there other children in your home who will also need instructional time?

Once all of these questions have all been answered, the parent will better know how to formulate the daily schedule. From our teaching experiences, we offer these considerations:

• For elementary age youngsters, always begin the morning with a brief discussion of such things as the day's date, the day of the week, the season of the year, the temperature, an overview of the day's lessons/activities. This helps struggling learners, particularly students with disabilities, be more aware of their immediate life and surroundings.

• Add in movement-type activities (e.g., activities in other rooms, physical activities, etc.) throughout your daily schedule so that students will not be tempted to become sleepy or lazy.

• Alternate academic lessons with non-academic subject lessons. For example, parents might open the day with a Bible or language arts lesson. The next period of instruction should probably be music, art, physical education, etc. This should provide a contrast in learning for the student.

• Students with more severe limitations in learning, attention, and/or behavior will need to have a greater amount of daily instructional time allocated for remediation, which means that there will be a lesser amount of time for regular instruction.

The final schedule should be written out showing the time each subject lesson is to begin, break times, play times, lunch, outings, and so on. The schedule should be posted in a prominent place in the home classroom and followed as closely as possible (Let your answering machine monitor your phone calls so you can stick to your schedule!). Remember, the degree to which the parent follows the daily schedule will affect in the long-run the amount and quality of structure that is provided to the student. Above all, parents must remember that they are always a model of behavior (either acceptable or unacceptable) before their children. And children will naturally imitate some or all their parents' behavior along the way. It logically follows, then, that if parents consistently follow the daily schedule, they should expect students to reciprocate that consistency in submitting to the expectations of the daily schedule.

Evaluating School Work

One of the most important educational procedures for which home teachers will be responsible is evaluating ("grading" for conventional educators) their child's educational performance. Not only will children realize their success (or lack thereof) from proper evaluation of school work, but parents will benefit from the process by recognizing that they are making progress in meeting the needs of their children.

The first step in understanding how to evaluate struggling learners' school work properly is determining that you will *give your child a grade everyday* for each of the subjects that he studies and has lessons in. Consistent, daily evaluation and recording of the child's progress is one of the only ways that a parent can know whether the child is *really* learning. Evaluation may mean giving tests sometimes, but it doesn't mean that you have to give a formal, written test everyday. On the contrary, if you have just introduced a particular new skill (e.g., in reading, spelling, math, etc.) to your child on a given day, you certainly wouldn't give a written 25-question test that same day (although some would argue that this would be a form of "pretesting," which can be a good technique at times). What home teachers will need to do, though, is find some informal way of evaluating the child's degree of mastery of that skill, even though you have only spent one day teaching the skill.

One way to do this is to keep a mental count of the number of correct answers your child gives you from the oral questions that you may ask during the teaching of the lesson . Of course, we are making an assumption that you will be asking a number of oral questions as the teaching of the lesson progresses (see Chapter 8 on the importance of asking questions as an effective teaching behavior). For example, suppose a teacher asks approximately ten oral questions during the teaching of a particular spelling lesson, and the child misses only two. The child's success or mastery rate for that day's lesson, therefore, would be 80% (i.e., he answered 8 out of 10 questions correctly). This is a measure of success (i.e., a grade) that the home teacher would assign to the student for his academic performance on that particular school day.

Keeping a record of correct response rate to oral questions is only one way of measuring a child's academic performance. As you continue teaching (and reteaching) a skill on successive school days, you may decide to give the child some independent assignments and perhaps eventually full-blown tests to determine how well he is mastering the skill. Just as with oral questions, the home teacher will need to determine the child's percentage of success as she scores these other measures. We suggest that the teacher remain consistent in recording in the gradebook each day the child's *success rate* (or mastery rate). Regardless of the type of assignment that you are scoring, the success rate would mathematically be the number of correct answers divided by the total possible questions/items that the child has to respond to (reported as a percentage).

We recognize that this is a highly "quantifiable" system of measuring a child's progress (i.e., having to count the number of learning tasks a child performs successfully). For struggling learners whose progress may not be as obvious or as pronounced from one day or week to the next, we suggest that parents quantify the child's mastery of skills on a daily basis so that both they and the child will be able to see the steady and consistent progress that is happening. Quantifying successful learning tasks in children can be difficult to do sometimes, but it will be much easier if parents make sure that skills and learning tasks they teach the child can be *observed* (i.e., the parent can either see it, hear it, or both see and hear it).

How will the parent know when the child has reached "mastery" of a skill? Mastery, in essence, is a demonstration of how well the child has successfully learned the skill at hand and is typically given as a mathematical percentage (e.g., 75%, 90%, 100%, etc.). The mastery rate should be determined and stated in advance by the parent, perhaps under the advisement of a special education consultant, if you are working with one. Determining the mastery rate for a skill will vary and requires that the parent carefully consider both the severity of the child's learning problem or disability and the type of skill that is being taught.

For students with moderate to severe retardation, for example, mastery of a particular skill may only mean from 75% to 90% accuracy. Yet for students who have mild learning problems or mild forms of disability (e.g., learning disability or attention deficit disorder), mastery may mean from 90% to 100% accuracy in a particular skill. Generally, parents should require higher percentage rates for *basic skills* such as reading functional sight words or calculating arithmetic problems using any one of the four basic operations. When more advanced reading, writing, and math skills are being taught, the chosen mastery rate might be somewhat lower.

We believe that a child has reached his individual mastery rate for a skill when he can score the stated percentage rate and sustain it for at least *three* consecutive school days. Children with milder forms of disability will reach their mastery rates sooner than children with more severe disabilities. Whatever the case, home teachers must exercise patience and faithfully continue teaching and reteaching the skill until the child can show the percentage goal for at least three school days in succession. In order to prevent regression in learning, parents will need to review the skill periodically as other new skills are introduced. Flynn[1] contends that home teachers will "want to aim for improvement, not necessarily mastery [for]....Mastery can discourage you because it takes...special children so long to get there." Parents who have children with more severe learning, attention, and/or behavior difficulties may certainly need to consider this when children are not able to show absolute mastery, even with repeated presentations and trials of the skill.

Recording Child Progress

Careful record-keeping is important in many areas of our lives, and we must not underestimate the importance of proper record-keeping in documenting the progress of our children in home education efforts.[2] The Home School Legal Defense Association[3] strongly urges parents to "keep accurate records that explain how you met [the child's] needs and how your child has progressed." Given the volatility of the disability rights movement in America and the increasing attention of government to the education of disabled students, we believe that careful record-keeping is especially important for home educators who have children with learning difficulties or disabilities. We recommend that, for each lesson/subject area, the home teacher's "gradebook" should include a daily record of the following:

(1) date;
(2) IEP objective (if an IEP is being used);
(3) specific skill/lesson;
(4) measure/form of evaluation; and → oral or written
(5) student's accuracy/percentage rate.

A simple spiral notebook or ring-binder would suffice as a gradebook. The home teacher might consider setting up the five categories above in a horizontal and vertical format as follows for easy, at-a-glance review of the student's performance for an individual lesson. Consider the example provided in Figure 11.2.

In this example, the parent has taught her child a math skill (counting by tens) that was required on the child's IEP. The parent used oral questions (OQ) as the form of evaluation. After she taught the lesson (which included carefully modeling how to count by ten), she gave her child five attempts to count orally by ten up

---

Figure 11.2

Gradebook Entry

Date	IEP Objective	Skill/Lesson	Measure	Percentage
2-18-95	Math #3	Counting/10s	OQ	80%

to one hundred on his own. The student was able to do so accurately four out of the five attempts, for a percentage success rate of 80%.

For brevity and convenience, the home teacher may choose to devise a coding system for identifying the IEP objective and the form of evaluation/measure. For example, the coding for evaluation/measure might be done this way: OQ=oral questions; TMT=teacher-made test; CMT=commercially-made test; TMWS=teacher-made worksheet; CMWS=commercially-made worksheet, and so on.

Developing a Permanent Folder

Conventional educators pride themselves in how they carefully document a student's progress through the school years. But then again, they must, because federal and state educational laws require that schools keep proper records on a child during his school enrollment. For many schools, a permanent folder is initiated when a child enters the school system, and this folder of information follows the child as he is promoted from one grade to the next through his school years. This folder will contain many documents that describe the child (i.e., physically, intellectually, academically, etc.) and changes that have occurred in his learning and behavior as time passes. We believe that home educators should also keep "permanent folders" on all of their children. It is particularly important to do so, though, if a child has serious learning problems or a bona fide, documented disability (see Chapter 2).

We have mentioned previously that the field of special education finds its roots in the volatile civil rights movement that ran so rampant in the 1960's and 1970's. Even today, one doesn't have to look far to find inordinate media attention directed toward children with unique needs. Pick up a newspaper on almost any given day or channel surf on the television only briefly and you'll find a "bleeding heart" for a child that has been disadvantaged or is challenged in some unusual way. Many of these children may, in fact, be disabled in some way. Our intention is not to appear to be insensitive here, rather we want to stress the importance of parents starting and maintaining proper paperwork on struggling learners who are being taught in the home. Failure to do so may draw unnecessary and potentially intrusive attention from local educational officials, child service agencies, and/or the like.

For students with documented forms of disability, we suggest that the home school permanent folder contain at least the following documents:

- basic demographic/background information
- initial psychological/psychoeducational evaluation report
- follow-up trienniel psyhological/psychoeducational reports
- physical exam results showing child in good health
- vision/hearing results
- diagnostic academic skill test results
- annual one-on-one achievement results
- individual educational plan (IEP)
- record of related services (e.g., speech/language, physical therapy, etc.)
- record of contacts and/or recommendations from special education consultant(s)
- copies of former and present final grades
- record of parents' final observations/evaluation of child's progress

These items should be stored in a safe place and updated regularly. Parents might consider having the special education consultant or other close, home educating neighbor keep duplicate copies of permanent folder contents.

---

[1]Flynn (1994), p. 43
[2]Lapish (1994)
[3]HSLDA (no date), p. 1

MANAGING STUDENT BEHAVIOR

Parents want their children to be well-behaved at all times, but the inherited sin nature (See Chapter 3) that children are born with simply will not allow this to happen. The sin nature produces many wicked, unrighteous acts of misbehavior throughout a child's lifetime. Since all children are born with a sin nature, there will be times of misbehavior for all children, whether they have a disability or not. Children will not always pay attention as they should. They will not always stay on-task and achieve in their school work as they should. They will not always complete their work with efficiency and success as they should, and so on.

For students with disabilities, there will be more frequent occasions of these undesirable behaviors. In addition to problems that stem from their sin natures, they will have characteristic behavior problems that generally accompany their disabilities (See Chapter 2). Managing student behavior, then, is a skill that is important for all parents, but probably more so for parents who have disabled children or struggling learners. C. Michael Nelson,[1] a leader in the field of behavior management, contends that unless teachers effectively manage the behavior of children, then optimal, effective learning will probably not occur. It behooves parents, then, to gain knowledge of and become proficient in implementing various behavior management techniques.

We begin this chapter with a discussion of some *preventative* techniques. Next we present several *short-term* behavior management techniques that can be implemented "on the spot" when problem behaviors are first observed. We conclude with a number of *long-term* techniques that can be employed in the home for behaviors in children that linger or are slow at developing and improving. Appendix A provides a number of resources which address behavior management in children that parents may find useful.

Preventative Techniques

We know that we can prevent certain problems in our lives by exercising proper precautions. For example, auto mechanics admonish us to change the oil regularly in our automobiles in order to prevent major breakdowns in the engine. As responsible drivers, we must be careful to check the tires on our cars to make sure they have adequate tread for driving so that needless accidents will not occur during rainy or icy weather. There are numerous other "preventative" checks that we must give attention to as we operate vehicles. If we fail to incorporate these preventative measures in our lives, then there is a higher likelihood that accidents or problems could arise.

It is much the same with our health. We are told repeatedly by physicians and health authorities that we should keep our weight down, exercise consistently, take vitamins, have regular physical checkups, and so on. If we are careful to address these precautions, we are less likely to experience more serious, potentially life-threatening health problems later on in life such as heart attacks and certain forms of cancer.

Similarly, parents will need to implement preventative techniques in order to head off some problem behaviors in children. W. Camp and B. Camp[2] discuss a number of preventative behavior management techniques. Five in particular are helpful and applicable to parents who have children with disabilities or struggling learners.

Set up your classroom to encourage good behavior. It is imperative that parents consider where they will provide instruction for their children. It will be awfully tempting to allow children to do their school work in any room in the house, even the family room or bedroom. But for children with disabilities, it is important to provide an instructional environment that is highly structured, free from distracting stimuli, and conducive to learning and good behavior (see Chapter 11).

Parents may want to consider setting up a room in the home that will be used exclusively for school. Comfortable desks, tables, and chairs should be set up for children to do their work. Small white boards or chalk boards should be available for providing direct instruction. File cabinets or "cubby holes" for organizing and storing workbooks and materials should also be present in this room. These types of things will provide the necessary structure that children with disabilities need to learn and behave optimally.

Start lessons promptly on time. We have discussed in Chapter 11 the necessity of developing a daily routine and schedule with designated times for instruction, independent work, etc. We believe that a very important preventative behavior technique has to do with starting each activity on the daily schedule promptly.

The old adage, "Idleness is the devil's workshop" is so appropriate here. We must recognize that when we fail to start an activity on time, we may be giving our children the opportunity to misbehave or to think about misbehaving. Some parents may downplay the importance of this preventative technique by arguing that a few minutes will not make that much difference. But, oh, how it can! How much time does a child need to get up from his assigned place and begin meandering around the home or outside in the yard? We need to assist struggling learners as much as possible in maintaining their concentration and attention. As we start class on time and abide by the daily schedule, we can expect fewer distractions and behavior problems.

Tolerate some noise and movement. Some parents may grapple with this preventative technique at first glance. After all, our children should be perfectly quiet and still, right? This is simply not the case with children who have disabilities. We have discussed in Chapter 2 some of the accompanying behavior characteristics of children with disabilities. For example, we know that many disabled children will demonstrate excessive movement at times. They will tend to talk out at times, because they may lack appropriate self-control skills.

Although our goal is to reduce movement and talk out problems in these children as much as possible, we must recognize that we probably will not get these noise and movement problems down to zero rates. We are not suggesting that parents excuse away completely noise and movement problems. What we are saying is that we cannot expect perfection from children who have obvious, God-given imperfections and limitations in their learning and behavior. Parents must exercise a reasonable degree of tolerance in this area.

Keep behavior rules simple and clear. We recommend that home teachers consider these three ideas:

(1) Develop four to six behavior rules, stated in positive, age-appropriate terms and using as few words as possible;

(2) Write them on posterboard in flamboyant, attractive colors; and

(3) Post them in a strategic position where the child will be able to see them frequently.

The choice of behavior rules will vary based on the needs of the child. It is most important, though, that parents use wording that is brief and understandable to the child. Although "Remain seated unless you have permission to get up" is appropriate and brief enough for students in middle school grades, the language is probably too lofty for elementary-aged students. It may be that you have to use picture rules for younger children with disabilities who have severe language/reading difficulties.

The place to post the behavior rules is critical. We recall one conventional classroom teacher who was extremely selective in choosing the best place. Instead of arbitrarily posting the rules just anywhere in the classroom, she observed for several days to determine where her students would look the most when they were not engaged in their school work. She concluded that the ideal place was the little window on the classroom door, since this is where her students would often look to see if any of their friends were passing in the hallway. Another teacher determined the best strategic position to be near the clock on the front classroom wall.

Enforce behavior rules consistently. This can be a most difficult preventative technique to implement for any teacher. Most of us have problems in consistently living right, let alone having to make sure that our children are behaving correctly in a consistent manner. Although we will probably not catch every behavior rule infraction that our children commit, we need to be as consistent as possible in enforcing the rules that we have set up in the home.

Children with disabilities have more problems with consistent school performance than children who are nondisabled. It only stands to reason that in order to assist them in behaving consistently, parents will need to provide continual enforcement of behavior expectations. The more consistent we are at requiring these children to be responsible and accountable for behaving well, the greater the chance they will generalize good behavior to other contexts and settings in the years to come as they grow older and mature. As a preventative technique, we are reducing the probability that more serious behavior problems will occur in the future if we consistently enforce basic behavioral rules along the way.

Short-term Techniques

Short-term behavior management techniques are also referred to as "antiseptic" or "band-aid" approaches to managing student behavior. We call them "short-term" techniques for two reasons. First, they are short-term with regard to the amount of preparation time the home teacher will have to invest in advance in order to get the technique ready for use and implementation. Once the parent has mastered an understanding of these techniques, s/he only need exercise keen observation and retrieval skills in knowing when to implement a certain short-term technique.

Finally, we call these techniques short-term because the home teacher will not have to wait a long period of time (e.g., from several weeks to several months) to see the desired change in behavior. For the most part, if the undesired behavior is minor in nature (e.g., tapping pencil on desk) and not too deep seated, the parent should expect the behavior to change right on the spot if the short-term techniques are applied appropriately, confidently, and firmly.

Parents should consider implementing short-term techniques at the earliest occurrence, better yet at the onset of problem behaviors. One additional thing to keep in mind is that one short-term technique used alone may not be enough to get a problem behavior under control. Parents may need to implement several short-term techniques in succession during a single situation in order to see successful behavior change.

It is also important not to discount the effectiveness of any one short-term technique just because it may not seem effective when used only one time on one particular day. Parents may need to apply a technique on a number of different days in order to see the full effect of behavior change. How long a parent should apply short-term techniques will vary based on the nature of the problem and the severity of the child's disability. But it is certainly better to exhaust short-term techniques before considering more time-consuming and intensive long-term behavior management techniques. Consider the following short-term techniques.

Planned Ignoring With Praise. For minor problem behaviors, it is best many times to simply ignore the behavior while concurrently praising the child for something that he is doing correctly and well. Parents should expect the problem behavior to diminish soon thereafter. An explanation of why this short-term technique works is somewhat difficult. But it may well be that the child is so shocked that he has been praised for doing some seemingly menial task (e.g., sitting straight in his chair) that he forgets about the minor problem behavior.

Imagine a young boy sitting at his desk (obviously in deep thought and reflection over his school work!) and incessantly tapping his pencil. It is not unusual for typical teachers who have very low tolerance for any amount of noise or movement to reprimand a boy like this. In experimental studies, it has been shown that ignoring troublesome behaviors like pencil tapping while praising the student for doing something well is effective in causing the problem behavior to diminish.[3]

Proximity Control. There will be times when parents may need to leave a child alone momentarily in the home classroom to work independently on an assigned school task. The average child who is self-motivated will many times stay on-task and remain undistracted. For students with disabilities, though, behavior problems will inevitably ensue. A good way to get behavior back under control is for the parent to re-enter the room where the child was left alone to work and move near the student, positioning his/her body next to the child (i.e., in close proximity).

We find that when teachers do this, the mere presence of the teacher being near the student is enough to cause the student to pause and consider his unacceptable behavior and desist. No doubt the maturity, control, and authority that the parent possesses has a positive influence on the child and plays a big part in the immediate behavior change in the child.

We see proximity control used often by highway patrolmen. It is not uncommon to see drivers on a freeway speeding upwards to 65-70 miles per hour, not abiding by the posted speed limit sign of 55. Amazingly, these drivers will immediately reduce their speed at the mere sight of a highway patrol car in the general locale. We should expect to see the same type of behavior change in our children as we apply proximity control in the home.

Urge Child to Self-reflect. Parents should not assume that *all* inappropriate behaviors in disabled children stem from their sin natures (e.g., rebellion or deliberate disobedience). Some inappropriate and undesirable actions are characteristic behaviors of the disabling condition, for example, shoddy penmanship for learning disabled students or failure to concentrate for children with attention deficit disorder. Many times parents forget that struggling learners are not mature adults and may not always remember *why* they are to behave properly. For children with disabilities, who may indeed have documented short- and/or long-term memory problems or reasoning difficulties, times of inappropriate behavior may come more often.

The "urge to self-reflect" technique calls for the parent to go through a series of oral questions with the child. The number of oral questions will vary from one child to another and from one situation to the next. But the phrasing of each question should cause the child to pause and *reflect* momentarily on the inappropriateness of his actions/behavior. The series of questions should gradually lead the child to reconsider his behavior and improve.

Consider Janie, an elementary mildly mentally retarded young girl, who has doodled all over her math worksheet and has turned it in to her mother for evaluation. Janie's mother notices immediately the messy work and, while pointing to the dooled marks, asks her daughter these questions: "Are you pleased with how your paper looks?"... "Do you think this is appropriate?"... "Is this paper neat?"... "Do you remember what we learned yesterday about neat school papers?"... "How could you make this paper look neater?" Parents should allow the child (or prompt) her to give a clear "yes" or "no" response to each question. Even if the parent has to go through the entire series of questions, it should take no more than a couple of minutes.

Humor as a tension diffuser. No doubt there will be times during the day when the pressure of school work seems almost unbearable to children with disabilities. Children may lose their good attitudes and composure. Tempers may begin to flare. Such occasions can be short-lived, though, if parents understand how and when to use humor as a tension diffuser.

Imagine a young learning disabled girl, Jenelle, who has been working on trying to master her three spelling words for the day. She has been at it for 45 minutes. Her mother gives her a quiz to check her mastery, and Jenelle only gets 2 of 3 correct. Jenelle understands from a prior agreement with her mother that she has to continue repetitively writing and practicing each of the three required spelling words until all three can be written correctly at one quizzing. Jenelle's temper gets the better of her, and she begins grumbling, complaining, and finally just pouts. Jenelle's mother smiles at her and in a very light-hearted manner says to her, "Sweetie...you look as blown-up as a bullfrog!" at which time Jenelle bursts into a joyful laugh. The mother's act of using humor in this situation was a quick, on-the-spot way of breaking the tension of the moment and may have prevented a minor behavior in Jenelle from escalating into a more serious one.

Long-term Techniques

We call these techniques that follow "long-term" techniques for exactly the opposite reasons that we called the prior ones "short-term." First, they are long-term because the parent will need to invest considerably more time thinking and planning in order to get long-term techniques ready for implementation. Second, these techniques are long-term with respect to the amount of time a parent will have to wait to see the effect of behavior change. For example, waiting from several weeks to several months for long-term techniques to take effect would not be unusual. There are two major types of behavior management techniques that we will discuss in the paragraphs that follow—*enhancement* techniques and *reduction* techniques. Each reflects a different goal of behavior change.

Enhancement Techniques

Enhancement techniques are used to *increase* the rate of or maintain good, desirable, appropriate behaviors in our children. When a child does not do enough of a good behavior (e.g., correctly solving math problems, knowing how to ask appropriately for something), enhancement techniques should be implemented to help him learn how to do more of it. A common thread that runs throughout many of the enhancement techniques is the concept of *reinforcement*. According to Axelrod,[4] the most powerful strategy in managing behavior in children is positive reinforcement. Positive reinforcement comes in the form of rewards and positive consequences that we can give to children for demonstration of good behavior. Yet we will see later on that positive reinforcers can also be withheld from the child in order to reduce poor, inappropriate behaviors (i.e., reduction techniques).

Positive Reinforcement Programs. The simplest of the behavior enhancement techniques to implement, a positive reinforcement program consists of identifying one or more of the child's behaviors (no more than three, preferably just one) that need to be improved. The teaching parent should make sure that the child understands that he is not doing enough of a desirable behavior and that, as he demonstrates more of that given behavior (e.g., completing 15 items on a worksheet in 15 minutes rather than just five or six as he has previously been doing), he will receive a reinforcer/reward. Choosing the right types of reinforcers that are appropriate to the child's maturity level and ones for which he has a strong desire is key to the success of a positive reinforcement program.

Types of Reinforcers. There are six types of reinforcers that students will respond to during their formative years: tactile/sensory (e.g., cuddling, hugs, etc.), edible, tangible, token, activity, and social reinforcers. These are ordered so as to reflect the developmental level of children. That is, we should expect younger children to desire and respond primarily to tactile-sensory, edible, and tangible forms of reinforcers since they are more materialistic in nature. Yet we should expect older students and adults to respond more favorably to token, activity, and social types of reinforcers most of the time.

Social reinforcers are the highest level of reinforcer. As such, we should not always expect younger children, when they do well, to be sufficiently reinforced from just a verbal comment such as "Good work!" (social reinforcer). Generally, the typical young child is simply not mature enough to receive the subtle reinforcing effect of social reinforcers. However, we should expect older, more mature and independent functioning adults to respond to social reinforcers. For example, a supervisor on a job site should expect a subordinate worker to continue performing quality work upon receiving encouraging words such as "Good job!" from the supervisor. Although the worker does receive a token reinforcer (i.e., his paycheck) intermittently along the way, he doesn't need to receive his wages by the day (or the hour) in order to keep on working at optimal levels. The social reinforcer from his boss should be enough for the moment.

In order for parents to prepare children to be able to receive and respond to social reinforcers one day, however, they will need to couple a social reinforcer such as "Good work...I'm proud of you!" with each tactile-sensory, edible, tangible, token, and activity reinforcer delivered. If we do this consistently through the years, we should expect children, when they reach adulthood, to be able receive social reinforcers from authorities in their lives without having to have a lower form of reinforcer on a regular, frequent basis. Our heavenly Father in a similar way showers us with rich blessings while here on this earth, yet we will be expected one day to respond in a spiritually mature way to His words, "Well done, thou good and faithful servant" (Matt. 25:21).

Christian parents and teachers are sometimes reluctant to reward children for good behavior. Their rationale sometimes is that "doing right is its own reward." Although this idea appears spiritually sound at first, it is not necessarily in keeping with God's example to us in the Bible. A careful look into the Scripture reveals that God is a liberal Giver of reinforcers and rewards (i.e., blessings) to His children. Interestingly, the richer blessings from God were always contingent upon obedience to His Word.

God made provision for a number of different types of reinforcers and blessings in His Word, including edible rewards ("manna" in Ex. 16:4 and "harvest" in Gen. 8:22), tangible and token rewards ("spoil" in Prov. 1:13), activity rewards ("rest" in Lev. 26:34), and social reinforcers ("help meet" in Gen. 2:18; "companions" in Phil. 2:25; and "friends" in Prov. 18:24). We believe, therefore, based on God's example in Scripture, that parents should give rewards and reinforcers freely and frequently to children upon demonstration of good behavior.

Reinforcement Survey. In order for rewards to have the reinforcing power that they are intended to have, we must give reinforcers that are *desired* by the child. All too often parents and teachers try to make "sugar pops" and "M & Ms" work for every child, when in fact, all children don't necessarily have a liking for either one of these. When *we* choose the reinforcers to give a child for his good behavior, those reinforcers may or may not be desired by the child.

Parents would do well to administer the following reinforcement survey, a series of open-ended statements designed to determine the types of reinforcers a child desires and responds to best. Read the following sentence stems to the child and have him/her complete them in writing or tape record his responses (you may have the child give two or three answers in rank order):

1. My favorite adult is...
2. What I like to do with this person is...

3. The best reward anybody could give me is...
4. My favorite school subject is...
5. If I had some money ($5, $10, etc.), I would...
6. When I grow up, I want to be...
7. The person who likes me the most is...
8. Two things I like to do best are...
9. I feel terrific when...
10. The way I get money is...
11. When I have money, I like to...
12. Something I really want is...
13. I would please my teacher by...
14. The person I like most to give me rewards is...
15. The thing I like to do best in school is...
16. The activity I like to do best on weekends is...
17. If I did better in school, I wish my teacher would...
18. I would do my very best work if I knew I could get...
19. The place I would like to visit the most is...
20. When I am with my best friend, I like to...

After the child responds, analyze his responses to determine whether he desires tactile-sensory, edible, tangible, token, activity, and/or social reinforcers. Simply classify each of the child's answers, and you may find that the child may only like one or two types of reinforcers. It would be wise to administer this reinforcement survey about once per school month to see whether the child's desires are changing. See Appendix B for a sample reinforcement survey completed by one home educating father with his learning disabled, gifted/talented son.

Once you have a list of potential reinforcers, you can then decide which good behaviors (e.g., attention span, remaining in seat, answering more math questions, etc.) need to be increased and, hence, reinforced. A good rule of thumb to follow is to concentrate on no more than one to three good behaviors at one time. Any more than three behaviors may be too much for a parent to keep up with.

After you decide which behavior(s) you need to reinforce, then you must determine how much of the behavior the child must show you in a given time frame in order to receive the reinforcer. For example, you may have concluded that your son generally completes only 5 of 10 math problems successfully on a typical assignment. It may be that you decide initially that the child will receive the reinforcer if he can complete 6 or 7 problems correctly. Over the course of several weeks, you can gradually increase the number of math problems you want the child to complete successfully in order to receive the reinforcer. Keep increasing the behavior goal until you reach the terminal desired goal (e.g., 90% to 100% correct math problems).

Positive reinforcement programs work best when parents set reasonable, attainable behavior goals and when the reinforcer is given liberally and frequently. It is also important that the desired behavior is reinforced at *each* occurrence. Remember, our children are counting on us to be consistent in our promise of delivering the reward regularly and on time. Above all, the child should only receive the reinforcer *contingent* upon meeting the designated behavior goal (i.e., 8 of 10 math problems, remaining in seat for 5 minutes, etc.). To give the child the reward when he just gives his "best effort" or whenever you "feel" that he should get the reinforcer may result in you unintentionally reinforcing unacceptable behavior.

Token Systems. Giving tokens to a child for good behavior or work done well in school is much like an employer giving an employee pay for his work rendered on the job site. One of the great advantages of using token systems is that the child can trade in the tokens for a variety of different edible, tangible, and/or activity reinforcers, much like adults will use cash to purchase useful and needed items. Children will readily recognize the purchasing power of tokens in getting the specific reinforcer(s) that they desire the most, and they will work diligently and hard to get them.

Interestingly, the token in and of itself has no power. Tokens in a stored box, like cash in one's bank account, do little good in the actual reinforcing of the good behavior. Only when the tokens are exchanged for something desirable and useful do we see the powerful effect that tokens have on increasing appropriate behaviors in our children. It is important that parents consider the following steps in developing an effective token system.

1. Select a token. Examples of tokens would include stickers, checkers, tickets, smiley faces, points on a card, hole punches on a card, etc. Choosing what type of token will be issued is a critical first step and should be guided by a number of important principles. One, make sure it is *safe*. Two, the token should be *foolproof*. That is, the student should not be able to duplicate or counterfeit it on his own. Using common objects that can naturally be found around the home as tokens would not be wise since the child could in a moment of deception issue to himself additional tokens that he has not earned. One classroom teacher testifies that she cut one-inch square pieces of different colored construction paper to use as her token. Although she cut and issued less than a hundred tokens to use for one week with her students, she reports that, when the students were ready to trade-in their tokens only a couple of days later, the total number of tokens from the group of students had all of a sudden grown to several hundred. Clearly, the students were wrongfully counterfeiting the tokens and attempting to trade them deceitfully.

Three, make the token *durable*. Some children will save their earned tokens for long periods of time. Paper tokens, therefore, would probably not be the most durable material for a token. The same teacher described above who had the counterfeiting problem also had another problem in this area. The students in her class were middle school age, and the boys in particular would place their earned (and counterfeited!) tokens in their back pockets on occasion. Of course, after several days of perspiration, the construction paper tokens were becoming quite moist, mangled, and even discolored. Laminating the paper with plastic might have allowed these tokens to be more durable.

A fourth principle is that the token should be *inexpensive*. The bulk of money invested in a token system should not be in the token itself, rather in the back-up rewards and prizes that the student will be able to trade for the tokens. Finally, make sure that the token is *undesirable* to the student. This is important, because one of the advantages of a token system is the ease with which the parent can administer the token reinforcer for acceptable behavior right on the spot without it interfering with on-going instruction. One thrifty teacher reported that she chose old baseball cards that she had purchased inexpensively at a yard sale as her form of token. Unfortunately, she realized on the first day of her token program that the baseball cards were a bad choice. The boys in the class, upon receiving the token (baseball cards) promptly for meeting their individual behavior goals, wanted to stop immediately and read the description of the athlete that was printed on the backs of the cards. Needless to say, the token not only interrupted the teacher's lesson, but eventually caused a disruption as well.

2. Determine back-up reinforcers. Back-up reinforcers are the actual or real positive reinforcers for which the child will trade his earned tokens. These can be as varied in nature as your imagination and pocketbook will allow. Be careful to choose reinforcers that are desired by the child. It would be best to administer the reinforcement survey (described earlier) to get ideas of the types of reinforcers the child would like to have. It will be important to choose several reinforcers that will range in value from "basic need" items such as pencils, play time, using a calculator, etc. to "luxury" items that may include toys and trinkets that the child has indicated that he would love to have. Your pool of back-up reinforcers may cover the gamut of reinforcer types from tactile/sensory to social reinforcers.

3. Establish token-exchange prices. Setting trade-in prices is your decision alone, based on your observations of your child and his needs. We have provided an example of one home educating mother's token-exchange program in Appendix C. You should probably keep these four economic principles in mind as you set your prices:

1. The number of tokens per reinforcer should initially be small to insure immediate success for the student. Present the child with only a few "basic need" and "luxury" items at first, and let the price of the "basic need" items be less than that of "luxury" items;

2. As token-earning behaviors and earned tokens increase, gradually increase the cost of the back-up items and increase the variety of items from which the child may choose;
3. As the program progresses and the child's ability to earn tokens increases even more, bring in additional luxury items (which will in effect cause the child to use up his earned tokens quicker so that he will not be tempted to save them for later to perhaps "take a day off" from home school);
4. In the final stages, increase token prices of "basic need" items and lower the prices for luxury items.

4. Establish how and when tokens are exchanged. The specific back-up reinforcers and corresponding token prices should be posted in a very conspicuous place in the home. For those children who cannot read, using pictures of back-up rewards will be much more meaningful than words. Parents might consider designating one corner of a room as the "Token Trade-in Store." There should be frequent trade-in times in the initial stages of the program, perhaps several times a day for the first few weeks. As the child increases his token earning ability and progresses along, the trade-in times should be spaced out over longer periods of time, perhaps once in the morning and once in the afternoon. After several weeks, it might be good to reduce the trade-in times even more to once every other day, and finally wean the child to the point that he can go several days until he *needs* a back-up reinforcer.

5. Define rules for acceptable behavior(s) or task(s). Choosing which behaviors you need to improve in your child will again be your decision. It will be critically important, though, that you keep several principles in mind:

1. Choose only behaviors which are observable (i.e., can be seen) and measurable (i.e., can be counted);
2. Specify to your child the acceptable level of performance that you are looking for (e.g., remain in his seat 90% of the time, will complete 85% of math problems correctly);
3. Start with only a few token-earning behaviors, making sure you include some easy, attainable behaviors on the part of

the child—you probably should not address more than three different behaviors at one time;
4. Make sure your child possesses the prerequisite skills to perform the behavior acceptably before you begin.

6. *Field-test token program before implementation.* This can be done easily by observing the child over several school days and keeping a record of token points that he would be earning for certain behaviors. Be careful not to tell the student what you are doing. This will allow you to see how many tokens he would be earning if this were a real situation. You should be able to use this "experimental" data to assess the prices for back-up reinforcers that you have set and make adjustments accordingly.

A number of final recommendations will make your token programs successful. One, plan a time to teach your child what to expect from the token program and how it will operate. Give an example to him and model how the tokens will be delivered to him and how he will exchange his tokens for back-up reinforcers. Two, be careful to issue a social reinforcer (e.g., "Great job!") along with tokens each time. Finally, keep careful records of tokens issued and redeemed, perhaps in your gradebook. For more information, home teachers may be interested in securing one or both of the following recent publications, which are available from the ADD Warehouse (see Appendix A): *Home Token Economy: An Incentive Program for Children and Their Parents*[5] and *Behavior Management At Home: A Token Economy Program for Children and Teens.*[6]

Behavior Contracts. Since contracts are a natural part of our everyday lives, it follows that home teachers may want to employ this concept in managing behavior in their children. Although some "contractual agreements" in real life are verbal in nature, those contracts that are written tend to be more binding between the parties involved. So it should be with behavioral contracts that we make with a student. They should be written.

In order to facilitate the contractual process, it is probably best to negotiate the details and specifics of the contract with the child, given that he is of age to provide input about himself. The contract concept, like other behavior management techniques, must specify a behavior that needs to be improved, and a reinforcer that can be earned contingent upon demonstrating enough of the particular behavior.

Behavioral contracts for younger, elementary-age children will look noticeably different from those written for older adolescents. Contracts for children will have more age-appropriate wording and should be embellished with color and graphics. Contracts for older students, on the other hand, should be more legal-looking and plainer in appearance. Properly designed contracts must contain the following elements in order to increase the likelihood of behavior change:

- specific task or behavior spelled-out;
- student's goal to increase the behavior;
- consequence(s) of attaining or not attaining the goal;
- beginning time—time contract goes into effect;
- deadline for completion;
- specific positive reinforcer/reward;
- parent and child signatures (others, if desired);
- dates under signature (day contract signed); and
- record of progress/indication of contract completion.

Reduction Techniques

Since struggling learners will demonstrate both desirable and undesirable behaviors, it naturally follows that parents will need to develop and implement behavior management strategies that will address both goals of behavior change—increasing the good behaviors *and* decreasing the bad ones. Many parents and teachers prefer enhancement techniques like the ones described above since they emphasize the positive aspects of and positive consequences to behavior.

But what about times when children do too much of an unacceptable behavior, like pinching, hitting, or leaving an assigned area or task without permission? What does a parent do when preventative and short-term techniques have been exhausted and there is still no improvement? That's when we must employ *reduction* long-term behavior management techniques. Reduction techniques are used to decrease the rate of or to eradicate poor, undesirable, inappropriate behaviors. Reducing undesirable behaviors can be accomplished through the use of reinforcement or punishers. We will discuss four reduction long-term techniques: differential reinforcement, reprimands, time out, and overcorrection.

Differential Reinforcement. We have discussed using reinforcement as a means to increase good behaviors, but it can also be used as a means to help reduce unpleasant behaviors in a child. There are several ways that differential reinforcement can be applied. One has to do with reinforcing a child when he keeps a poor behavior at a designated low rate.

For example, consider a student who is having difficulty remembering to double-check his mathematics problems. The result is that he has a high rate of errors. His mother notes that, on each of the last three class days of 20-problem assignments, he has missed -10, -12, and -8 problems. The parent may set up an agreement with the child where he receives his reward only when he misses no more than -4 problems out of 20 (which would be an 80% success rate). This is called *differential reinforcement of low rate of response*. Of course, the success goal could be strengthened gradually over time by reducing even more the number of missed answers that would earn a reward.

Another form of differential reinforcement deals with giving a child a reward only when he demonstrates a behavior that is the exact opposite of the target problem behavior. For example, suppose a child is out of his seat constantly during a given 20-minute lesson. The mother instructs the child that he will receive a reward only if he remains in his seat the entire 20-minute lesson. "In-seat" behavior is totally incompatible with "out-of-seat" behavior. In-seat behavior is, in fact, the exact opposite of out-of-seat behavior, and in-seat behavior can only occur when out-of-seat behavior is not occurring. This is called *differential reinforcement of incompatible behavior*.

Reprimands. Reprimands are the mildest, most common and non-controversial form of punisher that can be used to reduce inappropriate behaviors. A reprimand is any expression of disapproval directed toward a child that may include:

1. verbal statements (e.g., Mother says, "Susan...please keep your mind on your school work.");
2. gestures (e.g., shaking finger, snap of a finger); and
3. facial expressions (e.g., scowling look, burning/staring eyes).

Generally, any one of these forms of reprimand used alone is ineffective. Parents can increase the chance that the reprimand will be effective by combining two or all three forms of reprimand at one time. For example, a mother might say with a scowling look, "Jason...please keep your mind on your school work," as she shakes her finger.

The manner in which the reprimand is delivered is also important. The reprimand should be given with *low intensity*. That is, the teacher's tone of voice should be firm, but not loud and/or out of control. By delivering the reprimand immediately when the behavior occurs (and when the child's behavior is only mildly disruptive rather than extremely disruptive), low intensity can be insured. The teacher should also deliver the reprimand in *close proximity* to the child. Distance between teacher and child only weakens the strength of the reprimand and increases the chance that the reprimand may be misdirected. Finally, a critical element of an effective reprimand is *contact*, either physically or with the eyes. Making direct eye contact with the child or slightly touching his shoulder will guarantee proper contact.

Time Out. Time out is considered to be one of the more severe forms of punishment. Time out occurs when a student is denied positive reinforcement (rewards) for a brief, specified period of time, not to exceed about five minutes. Initially, the child should be placed in time out from one to two minutes. As additional time out periods become necessary, the time out period can be increased. There are three simple forms of time out: (1) non-exclusion time out; (2) exclusion time out; and (3) isolation time out. The types of time out grow progressively more punishing. For example, isolation time denies the child more reinforcing opportunities than exclusion time out, and similarly, with exclusion time out to non-exclusion time out. Parents should begin with non-exclusion time out and gradually move toward the other two types, if the behavior worsens or persists. Each form of time out is defined and described below:

1. *Non-exclusion time out*—child is allowed to see and hear other brothers/sisters succeeding and receiving rewards while he continues with his school work and remains with the group, but he is not allowed to participate in reward-earning activities;

2. *Exclusion time out*—child is not only denied the privilege of participating in reward-earning activities, but he is not allowed to see other brothers/sisters getting rewards either, although he may be allowed to *hear* (e.g., Johnny is asked to turn his chair around so his back is facing the other family members, and he works by himself. He can only hear others.);

3. *Isolation time out*—child is completely removed from the teaching-learning situation, not able to see or be in the presence of others who are involved in reward-earning activities (e.g., Johnny is asked to go sit in another room in the home, completely separate from mother and brothers/sisters).

Giving careful attention to several considerations will make time out more effective. One, make sure that sending child to time out does *not* present him with an opportunity to avoid or escape an unpleasant task. For example, if a student is being uncooperative because he does not want to complete a difficult academic task, then sending him to time out only to allow him to return and do some school task that he enjoys is allowing him to avoid something unpleasant. Time out in this case will prove to be counterproductive. The parent should make it clear to the child that, upon returning to the learning situation, he will still have to complete the task that he was attempting to avoid by misbehaving and intentionally being sent to time out.

Two, do not administer time out as a substitute for a more aversive punishment that has been promised. This occurs when a parent has warned a child that, for example, he may have to do three hours of yard work if he does not correct his behavior, and then sends the child to time out instead. Finally, make sure that the environment of the time out setting is not more reinforcing that the reward-earning teaching/learning environment that you are removing him from. A parent who decides that a child should be placed in isolation time out and sends him to the family room (which may have a television, stereo, video games, card games, etc.) is providing a more reinforcing environment than was the teaching situation.

✓ **Overcorrection.** Overcorrection is the most recently developed form of punishment technique. Although typically used in institutional settings for individuals who aggressively destroy or deface property, it can be generalized nicely to home settings. Interestingly, there is a scriptural basis for overcorrection. In Leviticus 6:2-7, we read of instructions given to Moses by God concerning how he was to discipline those under his leadership who have sinned. The passage reads:

> *If a soul sin, and commit a trespass against the Lord, and lie unto his neighbor in that which was delivered him to keep, or in fellowship, or in a thing taken away by violence, or hath deceived his neighbor; Or have found that which was lost, and lieth concerning it, and sweareth falsely; in any or all these that a man doeth, sinning therein; Then it shall be, because he hath sinned, and is guilty, that he shall restore that which he took violently away, or the thing which he had deceitfully gotten, or that which was delivered him to keep, or the lost thing which he found, Or all that about which he hath sworn falsely; he shall even restore it in the principal, and shall add the fifth part more thereto, and give it unto him to whom it appertaineth...*

Simply put, God intended for a person who had committed a trespass to restore what was damaged or taken to its original state. But in addition to this, God instructed that the offender was to go beyond restoration of the principal amount and do a fifth (i.e., 20%) more.

This "restore-plus" principle found in the book of Leviticus is evident in the *restitutional* form of overcorrection used by some special educators today. Consider an angry student, who enters the classroom and who intentionally knocks over a stack of books on the teacher's desk. Restitutional overcorrection occurs when the teacher immediately instructs the student to place the books back on the desk in a stack as they originally were when he entered. In addition, the teacher may have the student clean all the erasure marks in all of those books, or perhaps clean and straighten all of the books on the book shelf in the classroom.

Sometimes viewed as another form of overcorrection, *positive practice* requires the student to perform a positive behavior correctly in a repeated manner. For example, consider a home educating parent has been working with her child in mastering the multiplication facts. However, there are several of the nine-family multiplication facts that continue to stump the child whenever multiplication problems (e.g., 3-digit times 2-digit) are given. Having the child repeatedly write and say the specific nine facts that he has not mastered (perhaps 30 times in succession) each time the error occurs in isolation or in an applied problem would provide him with the needed positive practice that would increase his mastery.

Summary

Several clarifications need to be made regarding the behavior managements that we have discussed in this chapter. One, we must recognize that teachers really do not "manage" a child's behavior per se. In reality, what we are managing are the child's environment and the various influencing factors and variables that directly affect the child's behaviors. More important, behavior management techniques are intended to influence a child's will to behave more appropriately.

Two, we must be careful to address both good and poor behaviors in our children. The temptation will be to employ the reinforcement/reward techniques described above, and steer clear of the techniques where unpleasant consequences or punishers are involved. Despite the growing philosophy in this world that unpleasant consequences to poor behavior should be avoided, it is clear based on the truth found in God's Word that this attitude must not be part of a Christian home educator's belief system. The Scripture reveals that along with the blessings and rewards in this life, there will be hard and unpleasant consequences for everyone.

So, it is with behavior management in the home. Simply focusing only on reinforcement of good behaviors while refusing to deliver unpleasant consequences (sometimes punishment) to a child for his unacceptable behavior will surely result in ineffective behavior management (and probably a very spoiled and selfish child). We wholeheartedly agree with Dr. Saul Axelrod,[7] one of the leading behavior management scholars, who has said:

> The preference that teachers have for reinforcement techniques over punishment is understandable and commendable. The conflict is that punishment procedures often work where reinforcement techniques do not. The failure to use punishment under these conditions can be contrary to a student's long-term best interests....It should...be understood that punishment is as natural a learning process as reinforcement. (p. 40)

---

[1]Nelson (1981)
[2]W. Camp & B. Camp (1989)
[3]O'Leary & Schneider (1987)
[4]Axelrod (1983)
[5]Alvord (1973)
[6]Parker (1995)
[7]Axelrod (1983)

APPENDIX A

Additional Resources

A to Z Guide to Your Child's Behavior
David Mrazek, M. D. & William
Garrison, Ph.D. with Laura Elliott
ADD Warehouse, No. 6302, $15

*ADAPT: Attention Deficit Accommodation
Plan for Teaching*
Harvey C. Parker, Ph.D.
ADD Warehouse, No. 0900A, $20

ADD Warehouse
300 Northwest 70th Ave., Suite 102
Plantation, FL 33317
(800) ADD-WARE

*The ADD Hyperactivity Workbook for
Parents, Teachers, and Kids*
Harvey C. Parker, Ph.D.
ADD Warehouse, No. 0954, $14

Goal Card Program
Harvey C. Parker, Ph.D.
ADD Warehouse, No. 0953, $15

Hands-On Equations®
Henry Borenson, Ed.D.
Borenson and Associates
P.O. Box 3328
Allentown, PA 18106
(610) 820-5575

Helping Your Hyperative Child
John F. Taylor, Ph.D.
ADD Warehouse, No. 3010, $20

Home Token Economy
Jack R. Alvord, Ph.D.
ADD Warehouse, No. 1975, $11

Independent Strategies for Efficient Study
Karen Rooney, Ph.D.
ADD Warehouse, No. 3501, $28

*Listen, Look, and Think: A Self-regulation
Program for Children*
Harvey C. Parker, Ph.D.
ADD Warehouse, No. 0955, $20

MotivAider
Steve Levinson, Ph.D.
ADD Warehouse, No. 4101, $90

*Nationally Challenged Homeschoolers
Associated Network* (NATHHAN)
Tom & Sherry Bushnell
5383 Alpine Rd. SE
Olalla, WA 98359
(206) 857-4257

The Notebook Organizer
ADD Warehouse, No. 0962, $16

Parents Are Teachers
Wesley C. Becker, Ph.D.
ADD Warehouse, No. 1974, $16

*A Parents Guide: Attention Deficit
Hyperactivity Disorder in Children*
Sam Goldstein, Ph.D. & Michael
Goldstein, M.D.
ADD Warehouse, No. 1566 $28
(pkg. of 10)

*The Parents' Hyperactivity Handbook:
Helping the Fidgety Child*
David M. Paltin, Ph.D.
ADD Warehouse, No. 1770, $28

Recordings for the Blind
20 Roszel Rd.
Princeton, NJ 08540
(800) 221-4792

Special Education: A Biblical Approach
Joe P. Sutton, Ph.D., Editor
Hidden Treasure Publications, $19.95
18 Hammett St.
Greenville, SC 29609
(803) 235-6848

Special Times (Quarterly Catalog)
Computer Software for Special
    Education
Cambridge Development Laboratory,
    Inc.
86 West St.
Waltham, MA 02154
(800) 637-0047
(617) 890-4640 in Massachusetts
Free subscriptions

Touch Math
Innovative Learning Concepts, Inc.
5750 Corporate Dr.
Colorado Springs, CO 80919-1999
(800) 888-9191

Why Won't My Child Pay Attention
Sam Goldstein, Ph.D. (video)
Michael Goldstein, M.D.
ADD Warehouse, No. 1562, $30

*Your Hyperactive Child: A Parent's
Guide to Coping with ADD*
Barbara Ingersoll, Ph.D.
ADD Warehouse, No. 0434, $10

APPENDIX B
Reinforcement Survey

1. My favorite adult is...*my father [and] my mother, because they take care of me and feed me and all that stuff!*

2. What I like to do with this person is...*I like to build Legos and I like...when they read to me...that's fun!...and building Legos...that's about it...hm...and we go camping and sometimes we go camping, not much...we go to the movies a lot!...of course, church, and that's fun...and then in the summers we do kid's crusades with clowns...we don't have too many vacations, but we have good vacations.*

3. The best reward anybody could give me is...*a trip to Israel with my parents and my sister and a Lego train set.*

4. My favorite school subject is...*history and then after that it would probably be science and then reading books independently would be number three.*

5. If I had some money ($5, $10, etc.), I would...*buy a Lego set and play with it, and play with it,...and play with it!*

6. When I grow up, I want to be...*a person who designs Legos and writes the little directions and stuff, because I have been doing it since three, and I think I would be very good at it, and...well...you know, that's kind of weird, or an architect, because I've been building since I was three, and I think I would be good at that, too!*

7. The person who likes me the most is...*I'm not really sure, because nobody doesn't like me, so everybody likes me, so I'm not sure who likes me the most because it would take me an hour to find out!*

8. Two things I like to do best are...*play Legos with my friends, and the other thing would be I like to play with Joseph and my friends.*

9. I feel terrific when...*I make my Dad proud of me, because that makes me feel good.*

10. The way I get money is...*I just sit down and wait for it to come on in!...[child joking with Dad]...Not!...well, I mow lawns to make money occasionally, and that's what I do, I mow lawns.*

11. When I have money, I like to...*first, I like to pay my tithes, so God doesn't get mad at me, and then I like to buy Legos or [G.I.] Joe's, and then play with my friends.*

12. Something I really want is...*to go to Israel with my family and friends, and family and friends, and relatives, and grandparents, and my friends*

13. If I had a chance to please my teacher, I would...*play music...instruments together at church, specifically trumpets, because I'm learning to play the trumpet...it's a dirty job, but somebody's got to learn how to play it! It would please my teacher a lot if I could do more independent work, so he could do what he does, and it would please him a lot if I could finish school each day a lot earlier.*

14. The person I like most to give me rewards is...*God, because He gives the ultimate, glorious rewards, and the glorious reward He could give me would be eternal life in heaven. And then the people on earth would be my parents, my mama and my daddy, 'cause I love them, and they love to give me rewards, and I love it when they love to give me rewards.*

15. The thing I like to do best in school is...*to read books or to have books read to me...[child sings] these are a few of my favorite things!*

16. The weekend activity or entertainment I enjoy most is...*having guests over and making very weird noises while having guests over.*

17. If I did better in school, I wish my teacher would...*finish earlier, and that would help a lot!*

18. I would do my very best work if I knew I could get...*[student could not give a response to this stem after many attempts by the parent].*

19. The place I would like to visit most is...*Jerusalem.*

20. When I am with my best friend, I like to...*play Legos, build forts outside, and play outside.*

Interviewer: Home educating father
Student: Gifted/LD son

APPENDIX C

Token Reward Exchange

Food Reinforcers (5 - 25 pennies)

- penny candy
- jelly beans/gummy bears
- lollipops
- marshmallows
- cookies
- kool-aid
- flavored ice cubes
- sodas
- ice cream
- restaurant meal

Activity Reinforcers (25 - 200 pennies)

- drawing markers/art
- television programs
- crafts
- ride on four-wheel motor bike
- shopping with mom
- baking cookies with mom
- swim at grandmother's
- fishing with dad
- sleep overnight at friend's
- video/Ninetendo game
- going to restaurant
- ticket to sports event/movies

Tangible Reinforcers (250 pennies)

- toy purchase

_____

LD Student-Age 5
Token: pennies

REFERENCES

Alvord, J. R. (1973). *Home token economy: An incentive program for children and their parents.* Champaign, IL: Research Press.

American Heritage Dictionary (2nd College Ed.). (1985). Boston, MA: Houghton Mifflin.

American Psychiatric Association. (1987). *Diagnostic and statistical manual of mental disorder* (3rd ed., rev., DSM-III-R). Washington, DC: Author.

Axelrod, S. (1983). *Behavior management for the classroom teacher.* New York: McGraw-Hill.

Becker, W. C., Engelmann, S., & Thomas, D. R. (1975). *Teaching II: Cognitive learning and instruction.* Chicago, IL: Science Research Associates.

Beery, K. E. (1989). *The Developmental Test of Visual-Motor Integration.* Cleveland, OH: Modern Curriculum Press.

Beechick, R. (1992). Hope for dyslexics. *Homeschooling Today, 1(2),* 45-49.

Behymer, M. E. (1993). Trainable and severely/profoundly mentally retarded students. In J. P. Sutton (Ed.), *Special education: A Biblical approach* (pp. 287-330). Greenville, SC: Hidden Treasure Publications.

Bender, L. A. (1938). *Visual Motor Gestalt Test.* New York: American Orthopsychiatric Association.

Bley, N. S., & Thornton, C. A. (1995). *Teaching mathematics to students with learning disabilities (3rd ed.).* Austin, TX: Pro-Ed.

Borenson, H. (1988). *The Hands-On Equations Learning System.* Allentown, PA: Borenson and Associates.

Brigance, A. H. (1983). *BRIGANCE Diagnostic Comprehensive Inventory of Basic Skills.* North Billerica, MA: Curriculum Associates.

Brill, R. G., MacNeil, B., & Newman, L. R. (1986). Framework for appropriate programs for deaf children. *American Annals of the Deaf, 131(2),* 65-77.

Brown, V. L., Hammill, D. D., & Wiederholt, L. (1986). *Test of Reading Comprehension: Revised Edition.* Austin, TX: Pro-Ed.

Brown, V., & McEntire, E. (1984). *Test of Mathematical Abilities.* Austin, TX: Pro-Ed.

Bullock, J. (1992). New Products: Touch Math (4th ed.). *Intervention in School and Clinic, 28,* 119-122.

Bullock, J. (1994). *Touch Math (4th ed.).* Colorado Springs, CO: Innovative Learning Concepts.

Bursuck, W. D., Rose, E., Cowen, S., & Yahaya, M. A. (1989). Nationwide survey of postsecondary education services for students with learning disabilities. *Exceptional Children, 56,* 236-245.

Cambridge Development Laboratory, Inc. (1995, Spring). *Special times: Special education software for grades K-12* [catalog]. Waltham, MA: Author.

Camp, W., & Camp, B. (1989). [Workshop on behavior management techniques]. Charlottesville, VA.

Carman, R. A., & Adams, W. R. (1972). *Study skills: A student's guide for survival*. New York: Wiley.

Clements, S. D. (1966). *Minimal brain dysfunction in children: Terminology and identification*. NINDB Monograph No. 3. Washington, DC: U.S. Department of Health, Education and Welfare.

Cohen, S. B. (1993). Effective instruction: Principles and strategies for programs. In B. S. Billingsley (Ed.), *Program leadership for serving students with disabilities* (pp. 169-252). Richmond, VA: Virginia Department of Education.

Connolly, A. J. (1988). *Keymath-Revised: A Diagnostic Inventory of Essential Mathematics*. Circle Pines, MN: American Guidance Service.

Council for Exceptional Children. (1994). Classroom tips for ADD. *CEC Today, 1(2),* 11.

Dunlap, J. M. (1994). Additional suggestions [Teaching children with special needs]. *The Teaching Home, 12(4),* 45.

Durrell, D., & Catterson, J. (1980). *Durrell Analysis of Reading Difficulty*. San Antonio, TX: Psychological Corporation.

Duvall, S. (1994, October). *The effects of home education on children with learning disabilities*. Paper presented at the National Christian Home Education Leadership Conference, Phoenix, AZ.

Ellis, E. S., & Lenz, B. K. (1987). A component analysis of effective learning strategies for LD students. *Learning Disabilities Focus, 2(2),* 94-107.

Engelmann, S. E., & Bruner, E. C. (1988). *Reading mastery: DISTAR reading*. Chicago, IL: Science Research Associates.

Engelmann, S. E., & Carnine, D. (1972). *DISTAR arithmetic III*. Chicago, IL: Science Research Associates.

Engelmann, S. E., & Carnine, D. (1975). *DISTAR arithmetic I*. Chicago, IL: Science Research Associates.

Engelmann, S. E., & Carnine, D. (1976). *DISTAR arithmetic II*. Chicago, IL: Science Research Associates.

Englert, C. S. (1983). Measuring special education teacher effectiveness. *Exceptional Children, 50,* 247-254.

Englert, C. S. (1984). Measuring teacher effectiveness from the teacher's point of view. *Focus on Exceptional Children, 17,* 1-15.

Englert, C. S., & Thomas, C. C. (1982). Management of task involvement in special education classrooms: Implications for teacher preparation. *Teacher Education and Special Education, 5,* 3-10.

Federal Register. (1977). *Procedures for evaluating specific learning disabilities*. Washington, DC: Department of Health, Education, and Welfare, December 29.

Fernald, G. (1943). *Remedial techniques in basic school subjects.* New York: McGraw-Hill.

Fernald, G. (1988). *Remedial techniques in basic school subjects.* Austin, TX: Pro-Ed.

Fichter, R. (1993). Learning disabilities. In J. P. Sutton (Ed.), *Special education: A Biblical approach* (pp. 211-252). Greenville, SC: Hidden Treasures Publications.

Flynn, G. (1994). Setting goals and reporting progress. *The Teaching Home, 12(4),* 43.

Fouse, B., & Brians, S. (1993). *A primer on attention deficit disorder.* Bloomington, IN: Phi Delta Kappa Educational Foundation.

Frankenburg, W., Dodds, J., Archer, P., Bresnick, B., Maschaa, P, Edelman, N., & Shapiro, H. (1990). *Denver II Screening.* Denver, CO: Denver Developmental Materials, Inc.

Garnett, K. (1991). Meeting the needs of children with ADD. *DLD Times, 8(2),* 4.

Gessell, J. K. (1983). *Diagnostic Mathematics Inventory/Mathematics System.* Monterey, CA: CTB/McGraw-Hill.

Gfeller, K. E. (1986). Musical mnemonics for learning disabled children. *Teaching Exceptional Children, 19,* 28-30.

Goldstein, S. (Speaker). (1989). *Why won't my child pay attention?* (Video). Salt Lake City, UT: Neurology, Learning and Behavior Center.

Good, T. L. (1979). Teacher effectiveness in the elementary school. *Journal of Teacher Education, 30,* 52-64.

Gordon, J., Vaughn, S., & Schumm, J. S. (1993). Spelling interventions: A review of literature and implications for instruction for students with learning disabilities. *Learning Disabilities Research and Practice, 8,* 175-181.

Greenbaum, C. R. (1987). *Spellmaster Assessment and Teaching System.* Austin, TX: Pro-Ed.

Hallahan, D. P., Hall, R. J., Ianna, S. O., Kneedler, R. D., Lloyd, J. W., Loper, A. B., & Reeve, R. E. (1983). Summary of research findings at the University of Virginia Learning Disabilities Research Institute. *Exceptional Educational Quarterly, 4,* 95-114.

Hallahan, D. P., & Kauffman, J. M. (1991). *Exceptional children: Introduction to special education (5th ed.).* Englewood Cliffs, NJ: Prentice Hall.

Hammill, D., & Larsen, S. (1988). *Test of Written Language.* Austin, TX: Pro- Ed.

Hammill, D. D. (1991). *Detroit Test of Learning Aptitude-3rd Edition.* Austin, TX: Pro-Ed.

Haynes, M. C., & Jenkins, J. R. (1986). Reading instruction. *American Educational Research Journal, 23,* 161-190.

Heckelman, R. G. (1969). The neurological impress method of remedial reading instruction. *Academic Therapy, 4,* 277-282.

Heuchert, C. M., & Long, N. (1980). A brief history of life space interviewing. *Pointer, 25,* 5-8.

Home School Legal Defense Association. (no date). *HSLDA's policy on home schooling children with special needs.* Paeonian Springs, VA: Author.

Houck, C. S., & McKenzie, R. G. (1988). *Paraprofessionals: Training for the classroom.* Circle Pines, MN: American Guidance Service.

Jones, B. (no date). *Chapel sayings of Dr. Bob Jones, Sr.* Greenville, SC: Bob Jones University Press.

Karlsen, B., & Gardner, E. (1985). *Stanford Diagnostic Reading Test* (3rd ed.). San Antonio, TX: The Psychological Corporation.

Kaufman, M., Agard, J. A., & Semmel, M. I. (1985). Methodology. In M. Kaufman, J. A. Agard, & M. I. Semmel (Eds.), *Mainstreaming: Learners and their environment* (pp. 21-53). Cambridge, MA: Brookline.

Kaufman, A., & Kaufman, N. (1983). *Kaufman Assessment Battery for Children.* Circle Pines, MN: American Guidance Service.

Kauffman, J. M. (1989). *Characteristics of behavior disorders of children and youth* (4th ed.). Columbus, OH: Merrill.

Kavale, K. A., & Forness, S. R. (1987). Substance over style: Assessing the efficacy of modality testing and teaching. *Exceptional Children, 54,* 228-239.

Keller, C. E., & Sutton, J. P. (1991). Specific mathematics disorders. In J. E. Obrzut & G. W. Hynd (Eds.), *Neuropsychological foundations in learning disabilities: A handbook of issues, methods and practice* (pp.549-571). Orlando, FL: Academic Press.

Kelly, L. J., & Vergason, G. A. (1985). *Dictionary of special education and rehabilitation* (2nd ed.). Denver, CO: Love Publishing Co.

Lambert, N., Nihira, K., & Leland, H. (1993). *AAMR Adaptive Behavior Scale- School Second Edition-Examiner's manual.* Austin, TX: Pro-Ed.

Lapish, M. (1994). Parent-directed therapy at home. *The Teaching Home, 12(4),* 42.

Larsen, S., & Hammill, D. (1989). *Test of Legible Handwriting.* Austin, TX: Pro-Ed.

Larsen, S., & Hammill, D. (1986). *Test of Written Spelling-2.* Austin, TX: Pro- Ed.

Leinhardt, G., Zigmond, N., & Cooley, W. W. (1981). Reading instruction and its effects. *American Educational Research Journal, 18,* 343-361.

Lerner, J. W. (1989). *Learning disabilities: Theories, diagnosis, and teaching strategies* (5th ed.). Boston, MA: Houghton Mifflin.

Levey, E. (1984). *Methods and materials for LD I.* Lecture notes from graduate course taught at East Carolina University, Greenville, NC.

Luckasson, R., Coulter, D. L., Polloway, E. A., Reiss, S., Schalock, R. L., Snell, M. E., Spitalnick, D. M., & Stark, J. A. (1992). *Mental retardation: Diagnosis, classification, and systems of support* (9th ed.). Washington, DC: American Association on Mental Retardation.

Luftig, R. L. (1987). *Teaching the mentally retarded student: Curriculum, methods, and strategies.* Boston, MA: Allyn & Bacon.

Markwardt, F. (1989). *Peabody Individual Achievement Test-Revised.* Circle Pines, MN: American Guidance Service.

McCarney, S. B. (1989). *Attention Deficit Disorder Evaluation Scale- Home/School Versions.* Columbia, MO: Hawthorne Educational Services.

McCarney, S. B. (1987). *Gifted Evaluation Scale.* Columbia, MO: Hawthorne Educational Services.

Mercer, C. D., & Mercer, A. R. (1981). *Teaching students with learning problems.* Columbus, OH: Merrill.

Mercer, C. D., & Mercer, A. R. (1993). *Teaching students with learning problems (4th ed.).* Columbus, OH: Merrill.

Mills, D. (1995). I.E.P.'s made easy. *NATHHAN News, 3(3),* 20.

Nelson, C. M. (1981). Classroom management. In J. M. Kauffman & D. P. Hallahan (Eds.), *Handbook of special education* (pp. 663-667). Englewood Cliffs, NJ: Prentice-Hall.

Nelson, R., & Lingnugaris-Kraft, B. (1989). Postsecondary education for students with learning disabilities. *Exceptional Children, 56,* 246-265.

Nowacek, E. J., McKinney, J. D., & Hallahan, D. P. (1990). Instructional behaviors of more and less effective beginning regular and special educators. *Exceptional Children, 57(2),* 140-149.

O'Leary, K. D., & Schneider, M. R. (1987). *Catch' em being good: Approaches to motivation and discipline* [video]. Englewood Cliffs, NJ: Prentice Hall.

Parker, H. C. (1992). *ADAPT: Accommodations help students with attention deficit disorder.* Plantation, FL: Specialty Press.

Parker, H. C. (1995). *Behavior management at home: A token economy program for children and teens.* Plantation, FL: Specialty Press.

Parker, H. C. (1990). *Listen, look, and think: A self-regulation program for children.* Plantation, FL: Specialty Press.

Parrish, S. (1995). Homeschooling the special needs child. *Homeschooling Today,4(2),* 42-46.

Patton, J. R., Beirne-Smith, M., & Payne, J. S. (1990). *Mental retardation* (3rd ed.). Columbus, OH: Merrill.

Psychological Corporation. (1992a). *Stanford Achievement Test* (8th ed.). San Antonio, TX: Harcourt Brace Jovanovich.

Psychological Corporation. (1992b). *Wechsler Individual Achievement Test.* San Antonio, TX: Harcourt Brace Jovanovich.

Psychological Corporation. (1991). *Wechsler Intelligence Scale for Children- Third Edition.* San Antonio, TX: Harcourt Brace Jovanovich.

Quay, H. C., & Peterson, D. R. (1983). *Revised Behavior Problem Checklist.* Longboat Key, FL: Author.

Reger, R. (1973). What is a resource room program? *Journal for Learning Disabilities, 6(10),* 609-614.

Reisman, F. K., & Kauffman, S. H. (1981). *Teaching mathematics to children with special needs.* Columbus, OH: Merrill.

Renzulli, J. S., Reis, S. M., & Smith, L. H. (1981). *The revolving door identification model.* Mansfield Center, CT: Creative Learning Press.

Richman, H, & Richman, S. (1993). *Guide to PA homeschool law* (5th ed.). Kittanning, PA: Pennsylvania Homeschoolers.

Robinson, S. (1987). Self-management: A tool for independence—A means of motivation, *LD Forum, 12,* 11-13.

Ruais, R. W. (1978). A low-stress algorithm for fractions. *Mathematics Teacher, 71,* 258-260.

Salvia, J., & Ysseldyke, J. E. (1995). *Assessment* (6th ed.). Boston, MA: Houghton Mifflin.

Scott, K. (1993). Multisensory mathematics for children with mild disabilities. *Exceptionality, 4,* 91-111.

Secord, W. (1981). *Test of Minimal Articulation Competence.* San Antonio, TX: Psychological Corporation.

Semel, E., Wiig, E., & Secord, W. (1989). *Clinical Evaluation of Language Function-Revised.* San Antonio, TX: Psychological Corporation.

Short, C. (1994). Teaching children with special needs. *The Teaching Home, 12(4),* 39-50.

Sindelar, P. T., Smith, M. A., Harriman, N. E., Hale, R. L., & Wilson, R. J. (1986). Teacher effectiveness in special education programs. *The Journal of Special Education, 20,* 195-207.

Somerville, S. (1994). Special education and the law. *The Homeschool ADDvisor, 1(1),* 1-2.

Stephens, T. M. (1977). *Teaching skills to children with learning and beahvior disorders.* New York: Merrill/MacMillan.

Strayer, D. (1994). What's our position on learning problems. *Homeschooling Today, 3(5) ,* 1.

Sullivan, P. M. (1982). Adminisration modifications on the *WISC-R Performance Scale* with different categories of deaf children. *American Annals of the Deaf, 122,* 62-69.

Sutton, J. P. (1993a, November). *How home schooling benefits special needs children.* Presentation delivered at the National Christian Home Educators Leadership Convention, Williamsburg, VA.

Sutton, J. P. (1993b). Is testing key in home school special education? *NATHHAN News, 2(1),* 6.

Sutton, J. P. (1994a). Room for growth in Christian education: Pleas from mothers of children with disabilities. *Christian Educators Journal, 34(1),* 16- 18.

Sutton, J. P. (Ed.). (1993c). *Special education: A Biblical approach.* Greenville, SC: Hidden Treasure Publications.

Sutton, J. P. (1994c). Standard curricula not enough for LD students. *NATHHAN News, 3(1),* 9.

Sutton, J. P. (1994d). Students with attention deficit disorder: Understanding and meeting their needs. *Homeschooling Today, 3,* 37-41.

Sutton, J. P. (1994e). Testing for ADD: Why it's needed, how it's done, and what if you can't afford it? *The Homeschool ADDvisor, 1*(3), 1-2.

Sutton, J. P. (1989). *The effects of grade level and program type on teachers' instructional behaviors in learning disabilities classrooms.* Unpublished doctoral dissertation, The University of Virginia, Charlottesville, VA.

Sutton, J. P. (1990). The forgotten sheep: Ministering to handicapped individuals. *BJU Voice of the Alumni, 64*(6), 7, 22-23.

Sutton, J. P. (1994f). When is a learning problem a learning disability? *The Teaching Home, 12(4),* 44.

Sutton, J. P., Everett, E. G., & Sutton, C. J. (1993). Special education in Christian/ fundamentalist schools: A commitment to *all* the children. *Journal of Research on Christian Education, 2(1),* 65-79.

Sutton, J. P., McKinney, J. D., & Hallahan, D. P. (1992). Effects of grade level and educational setting on behaviors of beginning learning disabilities teachers. *Learning Disabilities Research and Practice, 7,* 16-24.

Sutton, J. P., & Sutton, C. J. (1994). A "recorded" solution for special students. *Journal for Christian Educators, 11(5),* 7-8.

Sutton, J. P., Wayne, J., Lanier, L., & Salars, K. (1993, November). *Home schooling special needs children.* Panel discussion delivered at the National Christian Home Educators Leadership Convention, Williamsburg, VA.

Swanson, J. M., McBurnett, K., Wigal, T., Pfiffner, J. J., Lerner, M. A., Williams, L., Christian, D. L., Tamm, L., Willicutt, E., Crowley, K., Clevenger, W., Khouzam, N., Woo, C., Crinella, F. M., & Fisher, F. D. (1993). Effect of stimulant medication on children with attention deficit disorder. A "review of reviews." *Exceptional Children, 60,* 154-162.

Task Force on DSM-IV. (1993). *DSM-IV draft criteria, 3-1-93.* Washington, DC: American Psychiatric Association.

Taylor, W. L. (1953). Cloze procedure: A new tool for measuring reliability. *Journalism Quarterly, 30,* 415-433.

The Hands-On Equations Learning System. [Brochure.] (1988). Allentown, PA: Borenson and Associates.

Thorndike, R. L., Hagen, E., & Sattler, J. (1985). *Stanford-Binet Intelligence Scale.* Chicago, IL: Riverside.

U.S. Department of Education. (1991, September 16). *Clarification of policy to address the needs of children with attention deficit disorders within general and/or special education.* Memorandum to the Chief State School Officers from the United States Department of Education, Office of Special Education and Rehabilitative Services, Washington, DC.

U.S. Department of Education. (1992). *Fourteenth annual report to Congress on the implementation of Individuals with Disabilities Education Act.* Washington, DC: Author.

Vaughn, J. C. (1993a). God's mandate for special education. In J. P. Sutton (Ed.), *Special education: A Biblical approach* (pp. 15-45). Greenville, SC: Hidden Treasure Publications.

Vaughn, J. C. (1993b). Orientation for parents and teachers. In J. P. Sutton (Ed.), *Special education: A Biblical approach* (pp. 47-81). Greenville, SC: Hidden Treasure Publications.

Vergason, G. A. (1990). *Dictionary of Special Education and Rehabilitation* (3rd Ed.). Denver, CO: Love.

White, P. (1994). Demystifying attention deficit disorders. *The Teaching Home, 12(4),* 46.

Wiederholt, L., & Bryant, B. (1992). *Gray Oral Reading Test-3.* Austin, TX: Pro-Ed.

Wilkinson, G. (1993). *Wide Range Achievement Test-3.* Wilmington, DE: Jastak Associates.

Wolf, J. S. (1994). The gifted and talented. In N. G. Haring, L. McCormick, & T. G. Haring (Eds.), *Exceptional children and youth* (6th ed.) (pp. 456-500). New York, NY: Merrill.

Wong, B. Y. L. (1986). A cognitive approach to teaching spelling. *Exceptional Children, 53,* 169-173.

Woodcock, R. W., & Johnson, M. B. (1989). *Woodcock-Johnson Psychoeducational Battery Revised-Tests of Achievement.* Allen, TX: DLM.

Woodcock, R. W., & Johnson, M. B. (1989). *Woodcock-Johnson Psychoeducational Battery Revised-Tests of Cognitive Abilities.* Allen, TX: DLM.

Zacherman, J. (1982). Administration of a resource program. In J. H. Cohen (Ed.), *Handbook of resource room teaching* (pp. 253-273). Rockville, MD: Aspen.

Zimmerman, B. (1982). Developing an elementary school resource program. In J. H. Cohen (Ed.), *Handbook of resource room teaching* (pp. 115-138). Rockville, MD: Aspen.

SCRIPTURE INDEX

Author Index

SUBJECT INDEX

ABOUT THE AUTHORS

Dr. Joe P. Sutton

As a certified educational diagnostician, Dr. Sutton provides testing and consulting services to a national clientele of Christian/home educators who have children with learning, attention, and/or behavioral difficulties. He is a frequent speaker at state level home/conventional education conferences and has delivered papers and presentations at national conventions sponsored by the American Educational Research Association, the Association for Teacher Educators, the Council for Exceptional Children, the Council for Learning Disabilities, and the National Center for Home Education. He was awarded a generous fellowship grant from The University of Virginia in 1986 and completed his Doctor of Philosophy (Ph.D.) degree in special education in 1989. He holds two master's degrees in educational administration and special education (learning disabilities) as well as a bachelor's degree in mathematics education.

Dr. Sutton has published numerous articles, many appearing in leading Christian education and home education journals and magazines. In addition to co-authoring a book chapter on specific mathematics disorders, he is the guest editor of the seminal book to date on *Christian* special education, *Special Education: A Biblical Approach.* He is a member of several professional organizations including the Council for Exceptional Children, the CEC Council for Educational Diagnostic Services, and Phi Delta Kappa. He is registered as a special education consultant with the Home School Legal Defense Association and serves on the Advisory Board of Hidden Treasure Christian School in Greenville, SC, one of the few self-contained special education Christian schools for students with moderate/severe disabilities in America. During the fall and spring semesters, Dr. Sutton is associate professor and chairman of the Department of Special Education at Bob Jones University.

In 1992, he was included in *Who's Who Among America's Teachers,* which honors annually the top 5% of teachers nationwide. He was recently nominated for inclusion in the 1996-97 edition of *Who's Who in American Education.* Born in 1956 and reared by loving, Christian parents on a 200-year old family farm in eastern North Carolina, Dr. Sutton currently resides in Simpsonville, SC with his wife, Connie, and their three school-age sons, Jeremy, Jason, and Jared.

Connie J. Sutton

Mrs. Sutton completed her Bachelor of Science degree (B.S.) in English Education at Bob Jones University, Greenville, SC in 1978. She served as a junior/senior high school teacher in several Christian schools in eastern North Carolina for five years. She accepted her first special education teaching position in a public school for juvenile delinquent boys in 1984 and began her pursuit of a master's degree soon thereafter. While her husband was completing his doctoral work at UVA, Mrs. Sutton continued to gain additional experience in the Virginia public schools as a special education teacher for adolescent emotionally disturbed and behaviorally disordered students. She completed her Master of Arts in Education (M.A.Ed.) degree in special education from East Carolina University in 1989.

Mrs. Sutton is now assistant professor of education at Bob Jones University where she teaches undergraduate and graduate courses to young people majoring in special education. She has co-authored a number of articles that have appeared in leading Christian education journals.

Although she juggles an unusually busy schedule, Mrs. Sutton successfully meets the rigorous demands of university teaching while maintaining a warm, loving home for her husband and their three sons.